A list of the pronunciation symbols used in this text is given below in the column headed AHD. The column headed Examples contains words chosen to illustrate how the AHD symbols are pronounced. The letters that correspond in sound to the AHD symbols are shown in boldface. Although similar, the AHD and IPA (International Phonetic Alphabet) symbols are not precisely the same because they were conceived for different purposes.

| Examples | AHD | Examples | AHD |
|---|---|---|---|
| p**a**t | ă | b**oo**t | o͞o |
| p**ay** | ā | **ou**t | ou |
| c**are** | âr | **p**op | p |
| f**a**ther | ä | r**oar** | r |
| **b**i**b** | b | **s**au**c**e | s |
| **ch**ur**ch** | ch | **sh**ip, di**sh** | sh |
| **d**ee**d**, mill**ed** | d | **t**igh**t**, stopp**ed** | t |
| p**e**t | ĕ | **th**in | th |
| b**ee** | ē | **th**is | *th* |
| **f**ife, **ph**ase, rou**gh** | f | c**u**t | ŭ |
| **g**a**g** | g | **ur**ge, t**er**m, f**ir**m, w**or**d, h**ear**d | ûr |
| **h**at | h | **v**al**ve** | v |
| **wh**ich | hw | **w**ith | w |
| p**i**t | ĭ | **y**es | y |
| p**ie**, b**y** | cb | **z**ebra, **x**ylem | z |
| p**ier** | îr | vi**s**ion, plea**s**ure, gara**ge** | zh |
| **j**u**dge** | j | **a**bout, it**e**m, ed**i**ble, gall**o**p, circ**u**s | ə |
| **k**ick, **c**at, pi**que** | k | butt**er** | ər |
| **l**id, need**le**[1] | l (nēd'l) | | |
| **m**u**m** | m | | |
| **n**o, sudden[1] | n (sŭd'n) | | |
| thi**ng** | ng | | |
| p**o**t | ŏ | | |
| t**oe** | ō | | |
| c**au**ght, p**aw**, f**or**, h**or**rid, h**oar**se[2] | ô | | |
| n**oi**se | oi | | |
| t**oo**k | o͝o | | |

[1]In English the consonants *l* and *n* often constitute complete syllables by themselves.

[2]Regional pronunciations of -or- vary. In pairs such as **for, four; horse, hoarse;** and **morning, mourning,** the vowel varies between (ô) and (ō). In this Dictionary these vowels are represented as follows: **for** (fôr), **four** (fôr, fōr); **horse** (hôrs), **hoarse** (hôrs, hōrs); and **morning** (môr'ning), **mourning** (môr'ning, mōr'-). Other words for which both forms are shown include **more, glory,** and **borne.** A similar variant occurs in words such as **coral, forest,** and **horrid,** where the pronunciation of *o* before *r* varies between (ô) and (ŏ). In these words the (ôr) pronunciation is given first: **forest** (fôr'ist, fŏr-).

# Why Do You Need This New Edition?

If you're wondering why you should buy the third edition of *Building College Vocabulary Strategies*, here are seven good reasons!

1. Chapter Objectives have been identified to help you focus on key skills.

2. A focus on how learning happens and the importance of using a variety of learning strategies.

3. Restructured outline so the Multiple Choice questions are now the first exercise you will complete to help the transition from a basic knowledge level to higher level thinking in the exercises that follow.

4. A new Appendix that offers the answers to the multiple choice feature will help you monitor your progress and focus your attention on problematic areas.

5. Updated Dictionary feature including the addition of the etymology and antonyms for each word!

6. Additional Vocabulary Tips will help you with the connotative meanings of words.

7. New Vocabulary Words that provide a clearer understanding of the structural elements.

# Building College Vocabulary Strategies

## Third Edition

**Darlene Canestrale Pabis**

*Westmoreland County Community College*

**Arden B. Hamer**

Indiana University of Pennsylvania

**PEARSON**

Boston   Columbus   Indianapolis   New York   San Francisco   Upper Saddle River
Amsterdam   Cape Town   Dubai   London   Madrid   Milan   Munich   Paris   Montreal   Toronto
Delhi   Mexico City   São Paulo   Sydney   Hong Kong   Seoul   Singapore   Taipei   Tokyo

To my students who inspired and challenged me everyday;

to my parents and children who believed in me.—DCP

In loving memory of John and Helen.—ABH

**Senior Acquisitions Editor:** Nancy Blaine
**Development Editor:** Jamie Fortner
**Marketing Manager:** Kurt Massey
**Senior Supplements Editor:** Donna Campion
**Executive Media Producer:** Stefanie Snajder
**Digital Project Manager:** Janell Lantana
**Production/Project Manager:** Clara Bartunek
**Project Coordination, Text Design, and Electronic Page Makeup:** Nitin Agarwal/Aptara®, Inc.
**Creative Director:** Jayne Conte
**Cover Designer:** Suzanne Behnke
**Cover Art:** Kasza / Shutterstock
**Printer/Binder:** RR Donnelley
**Cover Printer:** RR Donnelley

This title is restricted to sales and distribution in North America only.

Credits and acknowledgments borrowed from other sources and reproduced, with permission, in this textbook appear on the appropriate page within text.

**Library of Congress Cataloging-in-Publication Data**

Pabis, Darlene Canestrale.
    Building college vocabulary strategies / Darlene Canestrale Pabis,
Arden B. Hamer.—3rd ed.
        p. cm.
    Includes bibliographical references and index.
    ISBN-13: 978-0-321-84425-5 (alk. paper)
    ISBN-10: 0-321-84425-4 (alk. paper)
    1. Vocabulary—Problems, exercises, etc.    2. Universities and
colleges—Curricula—Terminology—Problems, exercises, etc.    3. Learning
and scholarship—Terminology—Problems, exercises, etc.    I. Hamer, Arden B.
    II. Title.
    PE1449.P244 2014
    428.1—dc23
                                                2012033566

14  16

ISBN 13: 978-0-321-84425-5
ISBN 10:    0-321-84425-4

# Contents

# Preface

## Introduction and Purpose

An extensive vocabulary and the ability to decode unknown words are important for reading comprehension. We have designed this text to help college students attain both. Students will work directly with 171 words presented in the chapters. While learning the words, students will work with structural elements that will enable them to decode additional words. In addition to presenting vocabulary words, this text addresses vocabulary learning through memory and learning strategies. We hope that students will use these strategies to enhance their vocabulary learning and then transfer them to their learning in other courses.

## Special Features

As mentioned, one important feature of this text is the emphasis placed on students' word attack skills for future reading and learning. Therefore, the words are grouped by structural elements, and information is given to help students use word attack skills and strategies to unlock future unknown words.

When effective readers encounter new words, they use several strategies to decode the word without interrupting their reading. The words in the chapters are presented in that format. First the words are presented with their pronunciations (See and Say) because students' listening vocabulary is often more extensive than their reading vocabulary. Second, structural elements are identified and defined. Next, the words are used in sentences with clear context clues, which mirror how content-specific words are presented in textbooks. Finally, the dictionary definition is given along with other information about the word to help the student have a deeper understanding of the meaning and usage of the word. This strategy (SSCD: See and Say, Structural Elements, Context Clues, Dictionary) is explained to the student in the Learning Strategy section in Chapter Two.

The text also addresses students' vocabulary learning strategies. Chapter One includes information about memory, how to maximize learning, and how adults differ in the way they learn compared to the way children process new information. This information about learning is reinforced throughout the chapters with Memory Tips and Learning Strategies directed at vocabulary that can also transfer to the students' other classes. In Chapter One there are individual, small group, and whole class activities that the instructor can use in class, or assign as an out-of-class activity to help students understand their own learning and what they can do to make the most of their efforts. This information is presented in Chapter One as opposed to an Introduction because we want to emphasize the importance of students becoming independent in their word attack skills, vocabulary learning, and other learning situations.

## New to This Edition

The third edition of *Building College Vocabulary Skills* has many new features while keeping the same format that reviewers and users of the first and second editions have reported as beneficial for their students.

- A focus on how learning happens and the importance of using a variety of learning strategies.

- The Multiple Choice questions are the first exercise students complete and the answers are included in the back of the book. This is in response to suggestions by the reviewers as well as students using the text. This also reinforces the flow from a basic knowledge level to higher level thinking in the exercises that follow.

- In the Dictionary section there are several additions:
  - The etymology of each word is given in order to further encourage knowledge and use of structural elements.

- Antonyms are given for the words in addition to synonyms. This further expands the students' knowledge of the word as well as their vocabulary.
- More Vocabulary Tips (which help students with the connotative meanings of words) and Memory Tips are included in the Dictionary section.

- There are several changes in the words selected for each chapter. These changes were made to reflect a clearer understanding of the structural elements. Additional words were selected based on the SAT Most Common Missed Word lists.

There are also several additions to the Instructor's Manual:

- Five-minute Quick Teach ideas that can be used at the end of a class if there is extra time

- Pretests instructors can use to direct students' learning and motivation to learn

- PowerPoints that are available on the Pearson website

- For some chapters there are web addresses where the students can find videos to reinforce either their word knowledge or their understanding of the learning strategies.

## Chapter Organization

There are ten chapters, each with two parts, A and B. In each part there are seven to nine words presented. This is the optimal number for learning; any more per section would be too much for students to master. At the end of each chapter there are three or four Power Words with one set of exercises. These words do not fit the structural elements, but are either interesting or important words for students to know.

The outline for each chapter is:

1. Motivational quotation

2. Memory Tip

3. Learning Strategy

4. Part A and Part B that each contain:
   a. Words to Learn with pronunciations
   b. Structural elements with definitions
   c. Words presented in context with context clues emphasized
   d. Dictionary information including etymology, meaning, another sentence, synonyms, and antonyms
   e. Practice Exercises:
      i. Multiple Choice
      ii. Fill in the Blank
      iii. Correct or Incorrect?
      iv. Short Answer

5. Power Words

6. Chapter Review
   a. Extend Your Learning
   b. Expanded Word Forms
   c. Puzzle Fun

## To the Instructor

We hope that you will find this text enjoyable to use as well as significant to your students' learning and success. In this third edition there are ten chapters, each with two parts and additional exercises. We are hopeful that you will be able to complete the entire book in one semester with your students. Please see the Instructor's Manual online for some ideas for classroom instruction.

## To the Student

We enjoy words and language and hope that this is evident throughout this book. We also hope that you will "catch" some of this enjoyment and interest. We both have used this text in our classes with hundreds of students and have incorporated their input in this and previous editions. In addition to an interest in language, we also hope that you will "catch" our joy of learning. There is information in this book about how you can be most effective in learning new vocabulary. This information can be transferred to any new learning task, whether it is in a college course or on your job.

# Acknowledgments

We are grateful to Eric Stano for his support of this third edition and to Nancy Blaine and Jamie Fortner for their continued help. We also want to acknowledge our early connections with Pearson/Prentice Hall and thank Ray Mesing and Craig Campanella. Megan Germ was our first reader and offered many suggestions and useful feedback. We are honored that several instructors who have used the second edition in their classrooms were willing to take the time to give detailed and useful feedback. Their feedback and ideas were great and we have incorporated many of them in this third edition. The reviewers were: Diana Ferrell, Imperial Valley College; Laura Gritman, Tallahassee Community College; Dr. Elizabeth Price, Ranger College; and Adalia Reyna, South Texas College—Pecan. Our colleagues at Indiana University of Pennsylvania and Westmoreland County Community College always offer support. Finally, we are grateful to our families for their support, encouragement, and understanding of our obsession with this project.

# CHAPTER ONE

# Memory and Learning

*A teacher can but lead you to the door; learning is up to you.*

Chinese proverb

## CHAPTER OBJECTIVES

**After reading this chapter you should be able to:**

Understand the basic steps to remember information

Understand learning strategies and relate them to personal learning

Develop fundamental study strategies to learn college vocabulary

Transfer strategies to other content courses

## CHAPTER OUTLINE

**Part A Memory—Don't Leave Home Without It**

The Memory Process

Research Findings About Memory

**Part B Multiple Learning Strategies for Vocabulary and Beyond**

One Final Thought!

How to Use This Information

## Part A: Memory—Don't Leave Home Without It!

A challenge that most college students encounter early in their freshman year is the daunting, almost overwhelming, amount of material that is to be remembered and understood. One of the first skills that you should focus on is a systematic way of remembering. Memorization is a skill. The only way to improve any skill is by practicing, so memorization should be approached in the same way—practice! We will look at memory in three ways:

- understanding the process of memorizing by using a diagram
- providing seven steps to practice when trying to improve memory
- reading research that supports the need for a strategy for memorizing

### The Memory Process

**STIMULUS**   Stimulus is any information that is accessed through any of the senses: anything that you see, hear, touch, taste, or smell. How many stimuli are you experiencing right now? Do you know the color of the chair that you are sitting on? Did you hear the girl in the back row cough two times? Can you feel the carpet under your shoes? Do you see the notes your instructor wrote on the board? All of these are stimuli.

**SENSORY MEMORY (SM)**   Sensory memory is the holding area for all stimuli. The purpose of the sensory memory is to identify information that will be kept and to "forget" unnecessary information. Information stays

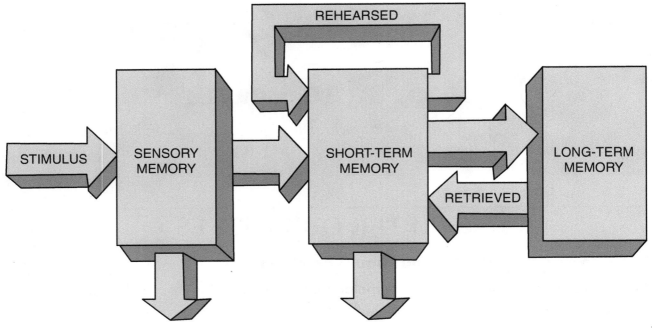

NOT TRANSFERRED TO NEXT STAGE
AND THEREFORE FORGOTTEN

in this holding area for a fraction of a second to a maximum of approximately four seconds. Duration is the term used to identify the amount of time that stimuli can be held. If you don't pay attention to the information, it is forgotten. If you do attend to the information, it is transferred to your short-term memory. Capacity is the amount of information that can be held in your sensory memory, short-term memory (STM), or long-term memory (LTM). The amount is measured in "bits." The SM and the STM can hold seven plus or minus two bits of information before you reach the overload mark.

*SHORT-TERM MEMORY (STM)*    Short-term memory is the working unit, a place where information/stimuli stay for a short time. The capacity for STM is the same as it is for SM—seven plus or minus two bits of information. The STM gives you another chance to keep the information or to forget it. If you decide to keep the information, your next task is to rehearse it so it can be transferred to your long-term memory. Rehearsal can be anything that involves thinking, writing, repeating, or retrieving to process the information. As you are rehearsing, or studying the information it starts to be transferred to the long-term memory.

*LONG-TERM MEMORY (LTM)*    The long-term memory is the holding area. This area holds all the information that has been stored throughout the years. The LTM has both unlimited capacity and duration; therefore, once information/stimuli get into the LTM they stay there indefinitely. Successful retrieval or remembering depends on how well you have filed the information. Filing of information in the LTM is crucial to successful retrieval. By creating connections with previously learned material, you create a hook of sorts that will help you to retrieve filed information.

Throughout your college career and beyond, you will appreciate the need for tools or strategies that will help you recall information. The following seven steps will help you improve your memory. We will return to these strategies throughout the book.

1. ***Intend to remember***—Sometimes this basic concept can be the difference between remembering and forgetting.

2. ***Organize the material to be learned***—It is easier to learn and remember information that is organized in a meaningful way.

3. ***Test/retest***—Restating information in your own words from memory will help the memorization process.

4. ***Over learn the material***—Making the information as readily available as possible is the goal, and that's what over learning will do.

5. ***Use memory techniques***—Being actively involved with the material, for example using visualization, association and mnemonics, promotes learning/remembering.

6. ***Space your learning over several study sessions***—The capacity of the STM dictates the need for several study sessions.

7. ***Study before bed***—Review before bed to minimize the effects of interference.

### Research Findings About Memory

Many memory experts feel that the major problem with remembering is not storage, but retrieval. Psychologists and educators have studied the effect of different learning strategies on students' ability to remember. Through research we know that learning takes place over time (space learning over several sessions), and it requires repetition, meaningful organization, association with what you already know, and practicing retrieval. At the most basic level, you need to make a conscious decision to intend to remember.

There are several factors that you need to know before deciding how best to learn information. How much do you already know about the subject? (The more you know the easier it is to learn new information.) How will the success of your learning be measured? What will you be asked to do with the information—straight recall, application to a new situation, relay minute details, or apply upper-level ideas and concepts? Finally, how long are you expected to remember the information—until the end of the semester or for use years later when you are working in your chosen career?

We also know through research that people differ in the ways that they prefer to interact with the information. The more ways you work with the information, the better you will understand and remember the material.

## Part B: Multiple Learning Strategies for Vocabulary and Beyond

To truly learn you have to go beyond memorization to understanding. How can you learn these new words and other information most easily? Here is a definition of learning that will help you figure it out:

---

Learning requires ***varied*** and ***repeated*** exposure to information ***spaced out over time***.

---

What does this mean in regard to learning?

- ***Varied***  Use multiple different strategies when working with the information; use different techniques and senses involving:
  - Vision
  - Color
  - Hearing
  - Your voice
  - Writing
  - Large and small muscle movements

- ***Repeated***  True learning and understanding does not happen in one setting; it takes many sessions.

- ***Spaced out over time***  New information takes time to become secure in your long-term memory; therefore, your studying needs to be spread out over an extended period of time.

### Exercises

Your instructor may assign one or more of these:

1. (Individual exercise) As you go through your day, keep a list of all the activities you do using the material you are learning for your classes, either in class or during your study time. Then:
   a. At the end of the day analyze these activities using the bulleted points listed below. Which involved color, voices, charts, writing, etc.?
   b. Next, look through the Chapter Review sections in this text at the various ways to Extend Your Learning. What activities can you add to your studying to help you learn better?
   c. Be prepared to share your thoughts with your class at the next meeting.

2. (Individual and small group exercise) Think about your hardest subject and list what you normally do to learn the information. How many different strategies do you usually use? When do you begin studying?

   Now get into a group of two or more. Share your answers and listen to what the others are doing. What strategies are they using that you can add to your studying? What strategies can you suggest to others that they might try?

3. (Small group and whole class exercise) Break into small groups. Each group chooses one subject that students in your institution commonly take and brainstorms how many different things you can do with the information to learn it. Consider strategies that use the different senses listed under the term *varied* above and the more specific strategies that follow. Share ideas with whole class.

Here are some specific suggestions for using one or more senses to make your learning more meaningful and your efforts more efficient.

Using your vision and color:

- Think in pictures.
- Use color. For example, write with different-color pens, highlight, use different-color papers.
- Make charts, graphs, concept maps.
- Make concept cards with written information and a trigger word(s).
- Read other material and watch for vocabulary words and structural elements.

Using your voice and hearing:

- Explain the information to others.
- Repeat the information out loud.
- Listen to tapes of recorded information.
- Listen to and be aware of vocabulary words and structural parts used in conversation, on TV, in movies.

Using large and small muscles:

- Write and rewrite.
- Manipulate the information by making charts, graphs, diagrams, etc.
- Make concept cards that you handle while you study.
- Role-play.

## *One Final Thought!*

You are now an adult learner and have different learning needs and goals compared to when you were a child. Here is the difference:

*ANDROGOGY VERSUS PEDAGOGY*    *Androgogy* is the term used to refer to adult learning, whereas *pedagogy* refers to the child as the learner. Knowles's theory of androgogy attempts to differentiate the ways adults learn from the ways that children learn. A number of assumptions are made based on this theory:

- Adults are self-directed.
- Adults are goal oriented.
- Adults are relevancy oriented (problem centered)—they need to know why they are learning something.
- Adults are practical and problem solvers.
- Adults have accumulated life experiences.

As an adult learner, you will use the preceding assumptions and the information you have learned about yourself to become a successful college student.

## *How to Use This Information*

Once you know how memorization and learning happen, what strategies work for you, and how to adapt learning to yourself as an adult, you can use this information in any learning situation to improve and/or enhance your chances for success. Remember to use multiple and varied strategies spaced out over time. Practice adapting these various strategies to different learning situations, materials, and requirements. Throughout this book you will find Memory Tips and Learning Strategies that you can use to enhance your vocabulary learning as well as your learning in other classes.

Enjoy!

Knowles, M. S., Holton III, E. F. & Swanson, R. A. (2005). The adult learner (6th ed.). London: Elsevier Inc.

# CHAPTER TWO

# Learning Words:
# A Strategy for Survival

*The true art of memory is the art of attention.*

Samuel Johnson (1709–1784)

---

## CHAPTER OBJECTIVE

**Students will be able to identify and use words with the following common structural elements:**

Roots: grate, greg
Prefixes: co-, col-, con-, cor-, com-
Suffixes: -ious

---

## CHAPTER OUTLINE

 **Memory Tip**    Intend to Remember

 **Learning Strategy**    SSCD, a vocabulary learning strategy

**Part A**
*Words to Learn*

| | |
|---|---|
| integrate | gregarious |
| segregate | superfluous |
| congregate | impetuous |
| egregious | |

*Structural Elements*

grate, greg
-ious

**Part B**
*Words to Learn*

| | |
|---|---|
| components | corroborate |
| contaminate | cohort |
| consolidate | conformist |
| collaborate | converge/ convergence |

*Structural Elements*

| | |
|---|---|
| co-, col- | con-, cor-, com- |

*Power Words*

| | |
|---|---|
| analogy | morale |
| notorious | immoral |

## Memory Tip    Intend to Remember

It is not enough just to "think" you will remember. You must make it happen. Begin with a conscious decision to intend to remember.

## Learning Strategy    SSCD

Many times words can be understood without going to a dictionary by following a simple strategy called SSCD.

*See and Say*
Examine the *Structure* of the Word
Use *Context Clues*
Consult a *Dictionary*

*SEE AND SAY*    Many students simply skip over unfamiliar words. By doing this you may compromise comprehension. Try to pronounce the unknown word. You may recognize the word from your receptive vocabulary and realize you already know it. When learning a new word, it is important to say the word out loud so that you hear it as well as read it. The more senses (hear, say, touch, taste, smell) involved in learning, the more long-term learning will occur.

*STRUCTURE*    This text provides you with the tools to use word parts to determine word meaning and also to see similarities between words. The general rule is to go from the known to the unknown. By looking at unfamiliar words and identifying word parts that you already know, you may be able to unlock the meaning of new words.

*CONTEXT CLUES*    Frequently there are clues to a word's meaning in the sentence and surrounding sentences. By using these context clues to determine meaning, you can quickly continue on with your reading without interrupting your comprehension. Chapters Three and Four give detailed information about the most common types of context clues.

*DICTIONARY*    Although you should always have a dictionary handy, try the preceding strategies before you interrupt your reading and turn to the dictionary. Also check to see whether your textbook has a glossary that will give you the definition specific to that area of study. Most dictionaries include multiple definitions, with the most common listed first. Be sure to select the definition that is the most correct in your sentence.

## Part A

*WORDS TO LEARN—SEE AND SAY*    Use the pronunciation guide on the first page of this book to help you SAY each word.

1. integrate          ĭn′tĭ-grāt′
2. segregate         sĕg′rĭ-gāt′
3. congregate       kŏng′grĭ-gāt′
4. egregious         ĭ-grē′jəs
5. gregarious        grĭ-gâr′ē-əs
6. superfluous      so͝o-pûr′flo͞o-əs
7. impetuous        ĭm-pĕch′o͞o-əs

*STRUCTURAL ELEMENTS*    Look at the structural elements of each word. Use these elements to unlock the word's meaning.

grate, greg              group, flock

-ious                       full of or characteristic of

*CONTEXT CLUES*   Read the sentences. Use the words around the unfamiliar word to determine the word's meaning. Words in bold are the vocabulary words; words in italic are the context clues.

1. The best teachers of young children **integrate** *play into learning*.

2. The army does not **segregate** *male soldiers from female soldiers*.

3. The study group decided to **congregate**, *or meet*, in the library's study room for one hour before class to go over their notes.

4. The star football player's **egregious** behavior was so *terrible* that it casued his teammates to remove him as captain of the team.

5. The college freshman was so **gregarious** and *liked being with other people* so much that she joined all of the clubs on campus.

6. Mike gave so much **superfluous** information in his essay answer that the professor couldn't find the correct information because of *all of the extra information*.

7. Tim's *sudden,* **impetuous** *reaction* caught everyone completely by surprise.

 *DICTIONARY*   Read the following definitions.

1. **integrate**   verb

   **Etymology:** in (into) grate (group or flock)

   To join with something else; unite; to make part of a larger unit

   It is very difficult for a person to **integrate** himself or herself *into a society* whose culture is different from his or her own.

   **Synonyms:** unite, combine

   **Antonym:** separate

2. **segregate**   verb

   **Etymology:** se (apart, away) greg (group or flock) ate (to make)

   To separate or isolate from others or from a main body or group

   The dormitory has always been **segregated**; *female students are on the first three floors while males are on floors four, five, and six.*

   **Synonyms:** isolate, separate

   **Antonyms:** join, unite

3. **congregate**   verb

   **Etymology:** con (together or together with) greg (group or flock) ate (to make)

   To bring or come together in a group, crowd, or assembly

   The campus security was concerned when officers noticed a *group* of young people who had **congregated** *in the middle of the street* and would not let cars pass through the campus.

   **Synonyms:** gather, assemble

   **Antonyms:** dissipate, disperse

4. **egregious**   adjective

   **Etymology:** e (out) greg (group or flock) ious (full of or characteristic of)

   Conspicuously bad or offensive

   It is an **egregious** act of *disrespect* for someone to *steal money* from groups such as the Salvation Army.

   **Synonyms:** flagrant, atrocious

   **Antonyms:** inconspicuous

**Vocabulary Tip:** Egregious has the root *greg*, which means "group or flock." The prefix *e-* (along with *ex-* and *ec-*) means "away from" or "out of." Therefore, the word *egregious* means that you have done something unusually bad and totally unacceptable by society that takes you "out of the group."

5. **gregarious**   adjective

**Etymology:** greg (group, flock) ious (full of or characteristic of)

Seeking and enjoying the company of others; sociable

As a four-year-old, Miles is very **gregarious** and *loves to play with other children.*

**Synonyms:** social, outgoing

**Antonyms:** antisocial, withdrawn

**Vocabulary Tip:** Originally this word was used to describe animals because animals usually live in groups, herds, or flocks.

6. **superfluous**   adjective

**Etymology:** superflo (overflow) ous (full of or characteristic of)

Being beyond what is required or sufficient

The traffic officer explained the directions to the hotel in *too much detail,* and the **superfluous** information confused the driver.

**Synonyms:** excessive, overabundant

**Antonym:** deficient

7. **impetuous**   adjective   *Personal behavie   (Think quickly)*

**Etymology:** impet (sudden or violent) ous (full of or characteristic of)

Characterized by sudden and forceful energy or emotion; lack of thought

Jerry's **impetuous** reaction to his coworker's error forced the department manager to suspend him for three days *so that he would learn to control* his anger.

**Synonyms:** hasty (but forceful), abrupt

**Antonyms:** deliberate, prudent

## *Practice Exercises*

### *MULTIPLE CHOICE*

1. What might someone do who wants to become <u>integrated</u> into a group of people?
   a. start dressing like those in the group
   b. say exactly what he or she thinks, don't be influenced by the group
   c. try to get the group to change its plans
   d. start his or her own group of friends

2. If a disruptive child is <u>segregated</u> from the rest of the children, he or she is
   a. moved to the center of a small group
   b. made the line leader for recess
   c. asked to pass out the reading books
   d. told to sit at a desk away from the others

3. Which of the following might <u>congregate</u> in an area?
   a. a group of protestors who want to make their cause known
   b. children playing hide and seek in a park
   c. several people each going their own way
   d. squirrels hunting acorns in the park

4. If a young boy committed an <u>egregious</u> act, what might be his parents' response?
   a. treat him to ice cream
   b. punish him by putting him in time out
   c. make sure that he is on time for school the next day
   d. tell him how to avoid punishment by being more secretive

5. Which of the following statements might a <u>gregarious</u> person make?
   a. "I want to be alone."
   b. "Let's call some more people and make it a real party!"
   c. "I prefer quiet dinners with just one or two other people."
   d. "I get my best work done alone."

6. How much money do you have if you have a <u>superfluous</u> amount?
   a. not enough to pay your bills
   b. more than you need
   c. just enough to make ends meet
   d. enough to pay your bills

7. An <u>impetuous</u> person's reaction to good news would be to
   a. jump up and down and tell everyone he or she sees
   b. write a letter home to tell his or her family
   c. calmly reflect on the news
   d. take a minute to thank the person who delivered the news

*FILL IN THE BLANK*   Select the BEST word for each sentence. Use each word only once.

| | | | |
|---|---|---|---|
| gregarious | congregated | superfluous | egregious |
| integrate | segregated | impetuous | |

1. When you are answering an essay question, you should try to __integate__ the information from the professor's lectures with the information you read in the textbook.

2. Jeannie felt that the extra time built into the schedule was __superfluous__ because she always had to wait.

3. Julie wishes that she was more __gregarious__, but she really preferred to sit at home and read her book while her friends went to parties.

4. During the unexpected thunderstorm, the students __congregated__ on the porch in order to stay dry.

5. The nurse __segregated__ the sick child from the rest of the students so that he would not spread his cold germs to the others.

6. The ~~impetuous~~ __egregious__ error changed the outcome of the game and cost the baseball team the championship.

7. At the preschool conference, the teacher told Lisa that her __egregious__ daughter never thought before she acted.
   __impetuous__

*CORRECT OR INCORRECT?*   If the sentence is correct, write a "C" on the line provided. If not, write an "I" for incorrect, then REWRITE each sentence to make it correct. You can change any part of the sentence to make it correct.

1. When she had an exam the next day, Judy did not like to study with a group of people. She always went to the study lounge where her friends were <u>congregated</u>.
   __I__ _____ not _____

2. Jim's parents were confident that he would spend most of his free time at college studying in the library because he was so <u>gregarious</u>.
   __Jim's parents were afraid that he would    (I)__

3. The <u>superfluous</u> information was just what Shelly needed to solve the problem.

_____

4. The Civil Rights Act of 1964 required states to <u>segregate</u> public school's, buses, and lunch counters.

_____

5. The senator's campaign plans were so <u>egregious</u> that he won reelection by a landslide.

_____

6. One goal of a coach is to <u>integrate</u> individual players into a single team where everyone works together.

_____

7. Chris was <u>impetuous</u> and thoughtful; therefore, it always took him a while to reach a decision.

_____

**SHORT ANSWER**   Write your answers on a separate sheet of paper.

1. Name three activities that a <u>gregarious</u> person might enjoy.

2. If you could have a <u>superfluous</u> amount of three things, what would they be?

3. List three reasons why a group of people would <u>congregate</u> in a room or building.

4. Name two groups or items that illustrate the concept of <u>segregation</u>.

5. If you have a child who is shy, how can you help him or her become <u>integrated</u> into his or her class?

6. Read the following scenarios. What would be an <u>impetuous</u> reaction to each?
   a. You pass your driver's test on the first try.
   b. Your boyfriend/girlfriend asks you to the prom.
   c. Your parents buy you a new car for your birthday.
   d. Your dog gets loose and runs away.

7. What is an <u>egregious</u> act at your school that is punishable with expulsion?

# Part B

🔊 **WORDS TO LEARN—SEE AND SAY**   Use the pronunciation guide on the first page of this book to help you SAY each word.

1. components            kəm-pō′nənts

2. contaminate           kən-tăm′ə-nāt′

3. consolidate           kən-sŏl′ĭ-dāt′

4. collaborate           kə-lăb′ə-rāt′

5. corroborate           kə-rŏb′ə-rāt′

6. cohort                kō-hôrt′

7. conformist            kən-fôr′mĭst

8. converge/convergence  kən-vûrj′/kən-vûr′jəns

*STRUCTURAL ELEMENTS*   Look at the structural elements of each word. Use these elements to unlock the word's meaning.

co-, cor-, col-, com-, con-        together; together with

 *CONTEXT CLUES*   Read the sentences. Use the words around the unfamiliar word to determine the word's meaning. Words in bold are the vocabulary words; words in italic are the context clues.

1. The course has four major **components**: *business law, finance, computing, and management skills.*

2. *Nuclear waste leaking into the lake* has **contaminated** the *purity* of the water.

3. To save money, the family **consolidated** their *many* credit card bills *into one* bill.

4. The CEO told his technical engineer that it is important to **collaborate** on the project *with someone* whose work ethic complements his.

5. The defendant's testimony was **corroborated** *by three witnesses*; therefore, the charges were dropped.

6. The **cohort,** *or group,* of students all progressed through their course of study together.

7. Stacey was a style **conformist** and *wore only the same styles* that her friends wore.

8. In Pittsburgh, PA, the Allegheny and Monongahela rivers **converge**, *or meet*, to form the Ohio River. At the **convergence** *point,* the city of Pittsburgh has built Point State Park and a huge fountain.

 *DICTIONARY*   Read the following definitions.

1. **component**   noun

   **Etymology:** com (together or together with) pon (put or place) ent (relate to or something that)

   A part that combines with other parts to form something bigger

   The factory supplies all of the electrical **components** *for the new cars.*

   **Synonyms:** element, part

   **Antonym:** whole

2. **contaminate**   verb

   **Etymology:** con (together or together with) tam (tag, to touch) ate (to make)

   To make impure or unclean by contact or mixture

   The letter was **contaminated** with *anthrax.*

   **Synonyms:** taint, pollute, corrupt

   **Antonym:** purify

   Vocabulary Tip: The word *contaminate* can also be used figuratively to describe the spoiling of a good thing, like one person's habit of gossiping that can contaminate a conversation among friends.

3. **consolidate**   verb

   **Etymology:** con (together or together with) solid (solid) ate (to make or cause to be)

   To unite into one system or whole; combine

   The two smaller classes were **consolidated** *into one large class.*

   **Synonyms:** merge, unite, combine

   **Antonyms:** segregate, break apart

4. collaborate   verb

   **Etymology:** col (together or together with) labor (work) ate (to make)

   To work together, especially in a joint intellectual effort

   To cooperate reasonably, as with an enemy occupation force in one's country

   *Dr. Smith and Dr. Jones* **collaborated** *on a nursing instructors' manual.*

   **Synonyms:** join forces, cooperate

5. corroborate   verb

   **Etymology:** cor (together or together with) robor (strength) ate (to make)

   To strengthen or support with other evidence; make more certain

   The lawyer had his clients statements **corroborated** *to be sure they were truthful* before they went to court.

   **Synonyms:** confirm, attest

   **Antonyms:** disprove, refute

6. cohort   noun

   **Etymology:** co (together or together with) hortus (garden)

   A group or band of people; a companion or associate; a generational group as defined by demographics, statistics, or market research

   The **cohort** of students made the test results clear for both faculty and adminintrators as *the group* all displayed the same results throughout the study.

   **Synonyms:** ally, supporter, associate

   **Antonyms:** opponent, rival

7. conformist   noun

   **Etymology:** con (together with) form (shaped) ist (something that or someone who)

   A person who uncritically or habitually acts in agreement with the customs, rules, or styles of a group

   Sam was such a **conformist** that he actually *bought the exact same car as his best friend.*

   **Synonym:** follower

   **Antonym:** nonconformist

   **Vocabulary Tip:** A conformist many times is identified as being negative because many believe that a conformist does not think for himself or herself.

8. converge   verb

   **Etymology:** con (together or together with) verge (to turn or merge)

   To come together from different perspectives or directions

   The scholarship team is planning to **converge**, *or meet,* in the administration suite to review the recent applicants for the presidential scholarship.

   convergence   noun

   The act, state, or condition of coming together from different directions

   The annual **convergence** *of the scholarship team* is planned to coincide with the deadline for applications.

   **Synonyms:** connect, unite

   **Antonyms:** disconnect, separate

*Practice Exercises*

*MULTIPLE CHOICE*

1. What would you do with <u>contaminated</u> water?
   a. drink it because drinking water is healthy
   b. pay for it because it is better than tap water
   c. not drink it because it might make you sick
   d. give it to your dog or cat

2. What is one <u>component</u> that is required for a relay race?
   a. several teams with several members on each team
   b. letting your friends know you are running
   c. cheering for the opposing team
   d. never practicing and always having a good time

3. Which of the following are characteristics of a <u>cohort</u>?
   a. move together as a group
   b. all follow the same rules
   c. each individual moves at his or her own pace
   d. all of the above
   e. both a and b

4. When would you need to <u>collaborate</u>?
   a. when you are preparing for your driver's test
   b. when you want to buy a new car and not have too big a payment
   c. when you are part of a group of bridesmaids planning a wedding shower
   d. when you want to share information that you wrote

5. To <u>corroborate</u> your neighbor's complaint that she made to the police about the neighborhood dog, you would
   a. tell about a similar event that happened with the dog
   b. describe an opposite chain of events
   c. ask further questions to be certain of her story
   d. take the dog to the animal shelter to protect it

6. Why would you want to <u>consolidate</u> your bills?
   a. because you have too many and want to reduce your monthly payment
   b. because you have too much money
   c. because you need to write more checks in order to qualify as a small business
   d. because you have to start preparing for finals

7. Which of the following statements would be made by a <u>conformist</u>?
   a. "I want to do my own thing."
   b. "I will do what everyone else wants to do."
   c. "Let's each do something different."
   d. "Let's think outside the box and change the rules."

8. Where might you find a <u>convergence</u>?
   a. in a quiet study lounge.
   b. at a dance where everyone is doing his or her own thing
   c. in a meeting to find a solution to a common problem
   d. in a brainstorming session planned to think of multiple ideas

*FILL IN THE BLANK*   Select the BEST word for each sentence. Use each word only once.

| | | | |
|---|---|---|---|
| contaminated | component | conformist | collaborated |
| cohort | consolidate | corroborated | converged |

1. One _component_ of learning a foreign language is to gain a basic understanding of the structure of the language.

2. Everyone in the room was ~~cohort~~ *contaminated* by Sally's cold germs when she sneezed repeatedly without covering her mouth.

3. The store manager _collaborated_ with other managers in the state to secure better benefits from the corporation.

4. The ~~contaminate~~ *cohort* all took the same classes during their course of study and graduated together.

5. At the school conference, the teacher told Megan that her son was a _conformist_ and followed the classroom rules to the letter.

6. Darlene _corroborated_ Tony's testimony when she told the exact same story about the night in question.

7. The student had so much information about his topic that it was difficult to _consolidate_ it into one half-hour speech.

8. The three small roads _converged_ to form a single main road.

*CORRECT OR INCORRECT?*   If the sentence is correct, write a "C" on the line provided. If not, write an "I" for incorrect, then REWRITE the sentence to make it correct. You can change any part of the sentence to make it correct.

1. The water in the stream was <u>contaminated</u> by the waste products from the nearby factory.

   _____C_____

2. The market analysist was interested in the <u>cohort</u> of people born between 1950 and 1970.

   ___C_____*at the same year*_____

3. One <u>component</u> of academic success is time management.

   _____C_____

4. After Jill and her professor <u>collaborated</u> on the research study, she earned a teaching internship at the university.

   _____C_____

5. If you <u>consolidate</u> your credit card balances, you will have more bills to pay each month.

   ___I_____*you will not have*_____

6. A <u>conformist</u> feels comfortable in a setting where there are very clear rules.

   _____C_____

7. Jim and Joe <u>corroborated</u> when they each told the police officer a different version of the accident.

   ___I_____*smiler*_____

8. Athletes from around the world <u>converged</u> at the opening ceremony to celebrate the opening of the Olympic Games.

   _____C_____

*SHORT ANSWER* Write your answers on a separate sheet of paper.

1. How does drinking water become <u>contaminated</u>?

2. What are two basic <u>components</u> that are necessary to be a successful leader?

3. Describe a situation in which you might be asked to <u>corroborate</u> with your daughter's version of events.

4. How would you begin to <u>collaborate</u> on writing a book report with your friend?

5. When you <u>consolidate</u> your lecture notes, what do you do?

6. Name five <u>cohorts</u> you belong to.

7. What are three benefits of being a <u>conformist</u>? What might be some negatives?

8. Draw a diagram to illustrate the <u>convergence</u> of five lines.

# Power Words

1. **analogy** ə-năl′ə-jē noun

   A statement showing the similarity between two things

   The following is an example of an **analogy**: *Your memory is like a muscle. The more you exercise it, the stronger your memory becomes.*

2. **notorious** nō-tôr′ē-əs adjective

   Widely known, but in a negative way

   The professor was **notorious** *for failing any student who was late to class.*

3. **morale** mə-răl′ noun

   The state of the spirits of a person or group as exhibited by confidence, cheerfulness, discipline, and willingness to perform assigned tasks; the general level of confidence or optimism felt by a person or group of people, especially as it affects discipline and motivation

   The *upbeat* **morale** of the enlisted men in the troop made the holidays more pleasant for the entire platoon.

4. **immoral** ĭ-môr′əl adjective

   Contrary to established accepted behaviors or principles

   Ashley was *always a well-behaved child; therefore,* when she started displaying **immoral** behavior, her *parents were shocked.*

## *Practice Exercises*

1. Complete the <u>analogies</u> using words from this chapter.
   a. Talk: speak :: group: <u>Talk is to speak</u> as group is cohort
   b. Infamous : notorious :: awful : <u>infamous is to notorious as awful is to egregious</u>
   c. Day : night :: pure : <u>Day is to night as pure is to contaminate</u>
   d. Integrate: segregate :: <u>as consolidate</u> : separate

2. Describe characteristics that would make a bank robber <u>notorious</u>.

3. Describe a situation in which a high school football team might have low <u>morale</u>.

4. Does your school have an academic dishonesty policy? If yes, why do you think the institution thinks it is <u>immoral</u> to cheat or use someone else's work?

## Chapter Review

### *Extend Your Learning*

Use one or more of the following exercises to practice the words in this chapter. Remember that it is important to use a variety of strategies in order to maximize your learning.

- Go to www.discoveryschool.com or a similar site and create a crossword puzzle.
- Take the words from this chapter and create rap/song lyrics as a way to remember the words.
- In other texts or articles, find at least five sentences that contain five different words from this chapter. Rewrite each sentence using a synonym for the vocabulary word.
- Go to www.easytestmaker.com or a similar site and create a multiple choice test for the words in this chapter.

### *Expanded Word Forms*

Select the appropriate word form for each of the sentences.

integrate          integrated          integration          converged          converging

convergence      consolidation      consolidating

1. The _____ of the four companies into one major conglomeration permitted all of the businesses to increase wages and benefits for their employees. By _____, the stockholders, employees, and consumers benefited.

2. Ryan had to _____ two software programs with a new one in order to accomplish his goal for the project. This _____ effort took over three months to accomplish but it yielded national acclaim. First he _____ the video elements and then the audio components before successfully completing the project.

3. Two protest groups received permits to march downtown at the same time on the same day. The police were very concerned about what would happen if the two groups _____ sometime during their marches. In order to try to stop them from _____, the police mapped out the march routes and tried to determine ahead of time the potential _____ points.

*Puzzle Fun*

**Across**

10. spirit
13. conspicuously bad or offensive
14. to make stronger by giving evidence to support an idea or story
15. a relationship that exists between ideas, words, etc.
16. contrary to accepted ways or manners
17. to isolate from others
18. beyond what is required

**Down**

1. to combine to tighten the unit
2. to come together from different perspectives
3. well known but in an unfavorable way
4. seeking and enjoying the company of others
5. to come together as a group, crowd, or assembly
6. a designated group of the same kind either in statistics or gender or other uniting factor
7. to make unclean or impure
8. make part of a larger unit
9. lack of thought
11. a person who uncritically or habitually acts in agreement to the customs, rules, or styles of a group
12. to work together as in a scholarly or other work-related project
14. part that combines with other parts

# CHAPTER THREE

# Using Words Properly—
# Right Time, Right Place

*One must be drenched in words, literally soaked in them, to have the right ones
form themselves into the proper pattern at the right moment.*

Hart Crane (1899–1932)

## CHAPTER OBJECTIVE

**Students will be able to identify and use words with the following common
structural elements:**

Roots: archy, arch, crat, cracy, pathy

Prefixes: omni-, pan-, hypo-, hyper-, an-, a-

## CHAPTER OUTLINE

 **Memory Tip**   Organize the Material

 **Learning Strategy**   Context Clues Part I

### Part A
*Words to Learn*

| | |
|---|---|
| hierarchy | panacea |
| archetype | pandemonium |
| monarch | aristocrat |
| omnipresent | democracy |
| omnipotent | |

*Structural Elements*

archy, arch

omni-, pan-

crat, cracy

### Part B
*Words to Learn*

| | |
|---|---|
| anarchy | hyperthermia |
| apathy | hypothesis |
| hyperbole | pathology |
| hypothermia | anomaly |

*Structural Elements*

| | |
|---|---|
| hypo-, hyper- | an-, a- |
| pathy | |

*Power Words*

| | |
|---|---|
| omnivorous | omniscient |
| panorama | anomalous |

## Memory Tip   Organize the Material

Organizing your room, your house, or your closet is a good example of why organization is important. Without having an organizational plan, locating what you need when you need it would be difficult and time consuming. This thought process is the same one that you should use for remembering. Retrieval, finding the information, will be easier if you begin to organize the new learning. For example, chunk your new vocabulary words into groups according to word parts, or in history be sure that you see the chronological order of the events you are studying.

## Learning Strategy   Context Clues Part I

This is the third step in the SSCD strategy—using context clues. Using the words around an unfamiliar word can lead you to an understanding relatively quickly. By doing this you will not jeopardize comprehension.

Several context clues will help you develop a basic understanding of unfamiliar terms. The most common context clues are:

1. synonyms

2. antonyms

3. direct definition

4. punctuation marks

5. examples

The following are examples of synonym, antonym, and direct definition. The other context clues are explained in the next chapter.

1. Synonym
   Because of his hubris, excessive pride, Jim would not ask for financial help from his parents.

---

Excessive pride is a synonym for hubris.

---

2. Antonym

   The car accident and resulting bills increased Sue's angst. She missed the peace of mind that she had before the accident.

---

The opposite of angst is peace of mind.

---

3. Direct Definition
   The witness's statement was so ambiguous, with so many meanings, that the police dropped all charges against Joe.

---

Having more than one meaning is the definition of ambiguous.

---

# Part A

*WORDS TO LEARN—SEE AND SAY*   Use the pronunciation guide on the first page of this book to help you SAY each word.

1. hierarchy           hī′ə-rär′kē

2. archetype           är′kĭ-tīp′

3. monarch             mä-närk

4. omnipresent          ŏm′nĭ-prĕz-ənt

5. omnipotent           ŏm-nĭp′ə-tənt

6. panacea              păn′ə-sē′ə

7. pandemonium          păn′də-mō′nē-əm

8. aristocrat           ə-′ris-tə-′krat

9. democracy            di-′mä-krə-sē

 **STRUCTURAL ELEMENTS**   Look at the structural elements of each word. Use these elements to unlock the word's meaning.

| | |
|---|---|
| omni- | all |
| pan- | all |
| arch | one who rules |
| archy | ruler |
| crat | one who rules or governs |

 **CONTEXT CLUES**   Read the sentences. Use the words around the unfamiliar word to determine the word's meaning. Words in bold are the vocabulary words; words in italic are the context clues.

1. The dancers were arranged in a **hierarchy** *from tallest to shortest.*

2. The sculptor made an **archetype** so that the client could see *a model* of the proposed statue.

3. All of the laws for the country were made by the *single ruler*, the **monarch.**

4. During finals week, students are **omnipresent** in the library. You can *see people studying all hours of the day and night.*

5. Because the king was **omnipotent**, he *alone had the power to decide* who would live and who would die.

6. Penicillin was considered a **panacea**, *wonder drug*, for most bacterial infections.

7. Since *all* of the children in the classroom were *talking at once*, **pandemonium** broke out.

8. The **aristocrats**, *those in the highest class*, decided what the current styles and trends were in the country.

9. In a **democracy**, the *people in power are elected by a general vote of all of the people.*

 *DICTIONARY*   Read the following definitions.

1. **hierarchy**   noun

   **Etymology:** hierarchia (ranked division) archy (lead or rule)

   A body of persons having authority; a series in which each element is graded or ranked

   Do you know *who is at the top* of the **hierarchy** in your school government?

   **Synonyms:** graded series, ranking

2. **archetype**   noun

   **Etymology:** arch (ruling or government) type (type or kind)

   An original model or type after which other similar things are patterned; a prototype; an ideal example of a type

   The structural engineer made an **archetype** of the building to present to the planning committee so they *could visualize the design.*

   **Synonyms:** model, prototype

3. **monarch**   noun

   **Etymology:** mon(o) (one) arch (one who rules or governs)

   One who reigns over a state or territory, usually for life and by hereditary right

   *Queen Elizabeth* is the current **monarch** of England.

   **Synonyms:** king, queen, ruler

   **Antonyms:** servant, employee

4. **omnipresent**   adjective

   **Etymology:** omni (all) present (present)

   Present everywhere simultaneously

   It seems that people who are texting are **omnipresent**; *everyone seems to be doing it all the time.*

   **Synonym:** everywhere

   **Antonyms:** nowhere, not present

5. **omnipotent**   adjective

   **Etymology:** omni (all) pot (power/strength/to be able) ent (relates to)

   Having unlimited or universal power or authority

   In the classroom, the instructor is **omnipotent**. *He or she decides* how the class will be conducted.

   **Synonyms:** almighty, supreme

   **Antonyms:** impotent, weak

6. **panacea**   noun

   **Etymology:** pan (all) cea (relates to)

   A remedy for all diseases, evils, or difficulties; a cure-all

   Scientists are trying to discover a **panacea** *for the common cold.*

   **Synonyms:** remedy, elixir

   **Antonym:** disease

7. **pandemonium**   noun

   **Etymology:** pan (all) demon (devil, evil spirits) ium (relates to, house of)

   Wild uproar or noise

   Students *cannot learn* when there is **pandemonium** *in the classroom.*

   **Synonyms:** chaos, riot, bedlam

   **Antonyms:** peace, calm

   **Vocabulary Tip:** It was said that in ancient times people who couldn't explain an uproarious event were heard saying that there was *pandemonium* occurring, which meant that "all the demons were called into the house."

8. **aristocrat**   noun

   **Etymology:** arist (the best) crat (one who rules or governs)

   A member of the ruling class or the nobility

   The **aristocrats** would *never consider staying in a regular hotel* room; instead they reserved a penthouse suite for their vacation in Miami.

   **Synonym:** elite

   **Antonym:** commoner

9. **democracy**   noun

   **Etymology:** demo (people) cracy (rule/govern)

   Government by the people, exercised either directly or through elected representatives

   One characteristic of **democrary** in the United States is that *we, the people, elect a president every four years.*

   **Synonym:** government

## Practice Exercises

### MULTIPLE CHOICE

1. Which of the following is arranged in a <u>hierarchy</u>?
   a. 20%, 35%, 50%, 75%
   b. 1, 4, 3, 5, 2
   c. apples, pears, oranges, bananas
   d. eggs, bacon, toast, orange juice

2. Which of the following would you find in a <u>democracy</u>?
   a. one all-powerful person making all the decisions
   b. government officials who listen to what the citizens want
   c. elections that are not held very often
   d. a small group of rulers who report to no one

3. You might build an <u>archetype</u> so that
   a. you would be done with the project sooner
   b. you could see what something would look like before making the final project
   c. no one would see your idea before it was completely finished
   d. you could keep your idea a secret

4. If someone is <u>omnipotent,</u> he or she is
   a. nowhere
   b. only seen occasionally
   c. very powerful
   d. all-knowing

5. Which of the following might characterize an <u>aristocrat</u>?
   a. never owned his or her own home or car
   b. able to trace family tree back to the queen of England
   c. used to doing what he or she is ordered to do
   d. none of the above

6. If you discovered the <u>panacea</u> for the common cold, you would
   a. be asked to teach at the local high school
   b. be fired from your job
   c. have repeated illnesses throughout the winter months
   d. be rich and famous

7. Characteristics of <u>pandemonium</u> are
   a. noise and confusion
   b. peace and quiet
   c. conversation and thoughtfulness
   d. organized games and activities

8. Which of the following statements is an example of something being <u>omnipresent</u>?
   a. "Can I borrow a pen? I can't find one anywhere."
   b. "Everywhere I look in my yard I see something else that needs to be raked, cut, or mowed."
   c. "I really want a blue backpack; can you help me find one?"
   d. "This semester is going very quickly."

9. What term would you use to address a <u>monarch</u>?
   a. Hey, you!
   b. Yo, buddy!
   c. Your Highness
   d. Dr. or Professor

*FILL IN THE BLANK*    Select the BEST word for each sentence. Use each word only once.

hierarchy    omnipresent    archetype    omnipotent    aristocrat
panaceas    pandemonium    monarch    democracy

1. The builder created a(n) _____archetype_____ so that the family would be able to see what their new home would look like.

2. The __aristocrat__ king made all the decisions for his subjects.

3. Some people would say that acetaminophen and ibuprofen are _____panaceas_____

4. The students were arranged in a(n) __hierarchy__ from highest to lowest grades on the exam.

5. A country that is a __democracy__ holds regular elections to decide who will be the leaders in the government.

6. If the inmates took over a penitentiary, there would be ____pandemonium____

7. Because his uncle was knighted in England, Sam always considered himself a(n) __omnipresent__

8. As __monarch__ King Julius ruled the country and made all decisions without consulting his advisers.

9. The family had three children under the age of six, so when you went into their house, toys seemed to be __omnipresent__ everywhere

*CORRECT OR INCORRECT?*    If the sentence is correct, write a "C" on the line provided. If not, write an "I" for incorrect, then REWRITE the sentence to make it correct. You can change any part of the sentence to make it correct.

1. The student grades were listed in a <u>hierarchy</u>; there was no special order.
   ____I/_____weren't_____

2. Because the form of government was a <u>democracy</u>, the people had no say in who the leader would be.
   _____could_____

3. The builder made an <u>archetype</u> of the shopping mall complex to facilitate the design for traffic flow.
   _____C_____

4. The toddler was <u>omnipotent</u> because his mother did not allow him to do anything he wanted.
   ___I/___wasn't_____

5. The <u>aristocrats</u> in the town lived in small houses and had to follow the orders given them by everyone else.
   ____I/_____

6. Because ~~none~~ of the test patients got better, the scientist knew he had created the <u>panacea</u> for the common cold.

   I / all of the _____

7. After his father, the king, died, Prince Juno became the <u>monarch.</u>

   _____ C _____

8. The new parents longed for the <u>pandemonium</u> that occurred only when their newborn went to sleep.

   I / _____

9. On our summer vacation seashells were so <u>omnipresent</u> on the beach that our daughter was hardly able to find any to bring home.

   I / _____

*SHORT ANSWER*    Write your answers on a separate piece of paper.

1. What is necessary for life? List six necessities. Put them in a <u>hierarchy</u>.

2. What would be the benefits of being governed by a <u>monarch</u> as opposed to living in a <u>democracy</u>?

3. What would be the benefits of living in a <u>democracy</u> as opposed to being governed by a <u>monarch</u>?

4. When might someone make an <u>archetype</u>? Describe a specific situation.

5. What is a synonym for <u>omnipotent</u>? An antonym? Write a sentence using the word <u>omnipotent</u>.

6. What are some benefits of being an <u>aristocrat</u> that you think you might enjoy? Any downside?

7. What could be a <u>panacea</u> for low test scores?

8. Describe a situation in which there is <u>pandemonium</u>. What might be happening? What is the atmosphere like?

9. List three things you would like to be <u>omnipresent</u> in your home or dorm room.

# Part B

*WORDS TO LEARN—SEE AND SAY*    Use the pronunciation guide on the first page of this book to help you SAY each word.

1. anarchy        ăn′ər-kē

2. apathy         ăp′ə-thē

3. hyperbole      hī-pûr′bə-lē

4. hypothermia    hī′pə-thûr′mē-ə

5. hyperthermia   hī′pər-thûr′mē-ə

6. hypothesis     hī-pŏth′ĭ-sĭs

7. pathology      pă-thŏl′ə-jē

8. anomaly        ə-nŏm′ə-lē

*STRUCTURAL ELEMENTS*    Look at the structural elements of each word. Use these parts to unlock the word's meaning.

| an-, a- | without; not |
| hypo- | under, below; less than normal |
| hyper- | over, beyond; excessive |
| pathy | feelings; disease |

*CONTEXT CLUES*   Read the sentences. Use the words around the unfamiliar word to determine the word's meaning. Words in bold are the vocabulary words; words in italic are the context clues.

1. Since the revolution gave way to **anarchy**, there was *complete confusion* and *no one was able to make decisions.*

2. Angie's **apathy** toward school became more obvious every day. She *didn't care* about completing homework, going to class, or taking exams.

3. When the professor said that his course was a "cake course" and *thousands of students got A's,* they knew he was using a **hyperbole**.

4. The doctor became very concerned about the young boy when he discovered that the boy was suffering from **hypothermia** *after falling in the freezing lake.*

5. **Hyperthermia** in its advanced state referred to as *heat stroke or sunstroke.*

6. Through several experiments, the scientist proved that his **hypothesis,** or *theory*, was correct.

7. The doctor knew from studying the **pathology** of the disease *what the progression would be and what was the best treatment.*

8. The **anomaly** that existed *between the twins* was that *one twin had blue eyes and the other twin had brown eyes.*

 *DICTIONARY*   Read the following definitions.

1. **anarchy**   noun

   **Etymology:** a/n (not/without) archy (govern, rule)

   Absence of any form of political authority; political disorder and confusion

   During the students' takeover of the campus, the *administrators were locked out of their offices,* and the result was total **anarchy.**

   **Synonyms:** chaos, disorder

   **Antonyms:** order, rule

2. **apathy**   noun

   **Etymology:** a (not/without) pathy (feeling)

   Lack of interest or concern, especially regarding matters of general importance or appeal; indifference; lack of emotion or feeling

   If you are depressed, you might *not really care* and have feelings of **apathy** about the day-to-day decisions you must make.

   **Synonyms:** disinterest, dispassion

   **Antonym:** interest

3. **hyperbole**   noun

   **Etymology:** hyper (over) bole (a throwing, a casting)

   Figure of speech in which exaggeration is used for emphasis or effect; obvious exaggeration not meant to be taken literally

   *"There were a million lights on in this house"* is a **hyperbole**. There are really fewer than twenty lights in the house.

   **Synonyms:** distortion, embellishment

   **Antonym:** understatement

4. **hypothermia**   noun

   **Etymology:** hypo (under) therm (heat/temperature)

   Abnormally low body temperature

**Hypothermia** in the elderly has grown to monumental proportions. *During the winter months* family and friends are encouraged to check on their elderly friends and family to be *sure they are warm enough.*

**Synonym:** subnormal body temperature

**Antonym:** hyperthermia

5. **hyperthermia**   noun

**Etymology:** hyper (over) therm (heat)

Unusually high body temperature

**Hyperthermia**, *high body temperature*, is the *opposite of hypothermia, low body temperature.*

**Synonym:** heatstroke

**Vocabulary Tip:** Hyperthermia is usually used when describing a medically induced increase in one's body temperature.

6. **hypothesis**   noun

**Etymology:** hypo (under) thesis (idea, point)

Something taken to be true for the purpose of argument or investigation

Sam's mother *tested* her **hypothesis** that he was allergic to wheat by not serving him any bread or wheat products for one week and then reintroducing them to him later to *observe the results.*

**Synonyms:** educated guess, assumption, theory

**Antonym:** fact

7. **pathology**   adjective

**Etymology:** path (disease) ology (study of)

(noun) The scientific study of the nature of disease and its causes, processes, development, and consequences

The **pathology**, or *scientific studies*, supported the doctor's recommendation that the patient stay on the same medication.

(adjective) relating to the scientific study of the nature of disease and its causes

The **pathology** *report indicated a mild bacteria infection* that could be treated with an aggressive treatment plan of antibiotics.

**Synonym:** diagnosis

8. **anomaly**   noun

**Etymology:** a/n (not/without) nomal (normal, even or same)

Deviation or departure from the normal or common order, form, or rule

The administrator was not able to explain the **anomaly**, *or difference*, between the school test results and those of the entire state.

**Synonyms:** abnormality, aberration, exception

**Antonyms:** conformity, uniformity

## *Practice Exercises*

### *MULTIPLE CHOICE*

1. Which of the following describes an <u>anarchy</u>?
   a. chaos, lawlessness
   b. calm, orderly

   c. police state

   d. tight control, methodical

2. You might feel <u>apathetic</u> if you

   a. had a specific goal in mind

   b. saw no hope for being successful

   c. were always trying to do your best

   d. were in a class with many of your friends

3. It would be difficult to believe a <u>hyperbole</u> because

   a. it would make perfectly good sense

   b. it would be greatly understated

   c. it would be a gross exaggeration

   d. it would understate the evidence

4. Which of the following does not mean the same as <u>anomaly</u>?

   a. offbeat behavior

   b. abnormal behavior

   c. unusual behavior

   d. ordinary behavior

5. What would you do with a <u>hypothesis</u>?

   a. try to prove it

   b. ignore it

   c. rewrite it

   d. correct the spelling

6. You would be interested in <u>pathology</u> if you were

   a. going on a vacation

   b. taking an exam

   c. sick

   d. learning how to sail

7. You might suffer from <u>hypothermia</u> if you were

   a. locked in the attic in the summer

   b. locked in a meat freezer

   c. denied water for 48 hours

   d. very energetic and drank caffeine

8. You might suffer from <u>hyperthermia</u> if you were

   a. locked in the attic in the summer

   b. locked in a meat freezer

   c. denied water for 48 hours

   d. very energetic and drank caffeine

*FILL IN THE BLANK* Select the BEST word for each sentence. Use each word only once.

| anarchy | apathy | anomaly | hyperboles |
|---------|--------|---------|------------|
| hypothesis | hypothermia | hyperthermia | pathology |

1. Sam found that his dog was suffering from _____ after being accidentally locked outside overnight in subzero temperataures.

2. All of Joe's test scores were above 90%, so the one score below 60% was a true _____.

3. The citizens knew the country was in a state of _anarchy_ when they could not tell who was actually in control of the government.

4. Judy was careful to have a full tank of gas before starting to drive over the desert in Nevada after she heard so many horror stories of people dying from _hyperthermia_ while walking in the heat.

5. The student approached his education with such _apathy_ that he never bothered to go to class or study for an exam.

6. In order to help his patients, Dr. Jeffers researched the _pathology_ concerning the rarest forms of cancer that he saw in his pratice.

7. When the lecturer finished, no one believed what he had said because of all the _hyperboles_ that went far beyond the stated facts.

*CORRECT OR INCORRECT?*   If the sentence is correct, write a "C" on the line provided. If not, write an "I" for incorrect, then REWRITE the sentence to make it correct. You can change any part of the sentence to make it correct.

1. Anarchy is an effective system of governing because citizens know that everything is under control and all their needs will be met.
   _I/D_ _____

2. Apathy was everywhere on campus, from classrooms to locker rooms, because of the excitement of the championship football game.
   _I_ _____

3. One way to avoid hyperthermia is to wear several layers of clothing in the summer to be sure that you are warm enough.
   _I_   _hypothermia_ _____

4. It is a hyperbole to state that all students do their very best work all of the time.
   _C_ _____

5. Sue was susceptible to hypothermia, so she moved to Alaska to avoid the problem.
   _I_ _____

6. The hypothesis that was stated in the thesis was proven incorrect by the evidence gathered.
   _C_ _____

7. The coroner had to seek additional information from the victim's doctors in order to determine the pathology of the disease and the cause of death.
   _C_ _____

8. My daugher's request to go to bed early was an anomaly, so I suspected that she was sick.
   _C_ _____

*SHORT ANSWER*   Write your answers on a separate sheet of paper.

1. Describe what a college campus in a state of anarchy might be like.

2. How would a professor act if he or she felt apathy toward his or her job and students?

3. Write a hyperbole about the landscaping on this campus.

4. Explain the definition of the word parts in hypothermia and hyperthermia.

5. Why would scientific inquiry be concerned with a hypothesis?

6. What would you try to learn about a disease if you were studying the disease's pathology?

7. What anomaly in a first grader's behavior might let you know he or she was having trouble in school?

## Power Words

1. omnivorous   ŏm-nĭv'-ər-əs   adjective

   Eating both meat and vegetables

   The black bear was **omnivorous** and would *eat small animals or plants* that he found in the forest.

   **Synonym:** voracious

2. omniscient   ŏm-nĭsh'nt   adjective

   All-knowing

   The kindergarten students thought their teacher was **omniscient** because she *always seemed to know* what they were doing and what they were thinking.

3. panorama   pa-nə-'ra-mə   noun

   An unbroken view of an entire surrounding area

   The **panorama** *of the entire countryside* from the hot air balloon was breathtaking.

   **Synonyms:** overview, perspective, diarama

4. anomalous   ə-nom'ə-ləs   adjective

   Deviating from the normal or common order

   The lawyer was trying to describe the **anomalous** characteristsics of the evidence *compared to the scientific data* in order to prove that his client was innocent.

   **Synonyms:** deviate, irregular

### Practice Exercises

1. Describe a meal that an <u>omnivorous</u> person would eat.

2. What is a synonym for <u>omniscient</u>? An antonym? Write a sentence using the word <u>omniscient</u>.

3. In your town or on your campus, where could you go to see a <u>panorama</u> of the area?

4. Describe three habits that are <u>anomalous</u> characteristics of an unsuccessful student.

## Chapter Review

### Extend Your Learning

Do one or more of the following exercises to practice the words in this chapter. Remember that it is important to use a variety of strategies in order to maximize your learning.

* Make a chart for the words in this chapter. Divide them into three categories: positive words, negative words, and neutral words.

* Get into a group and create a verbal "chain-letter story." Here's how: The first person picks one of the words from this chapter and creates the first sentence of a story. That person should write the sentence as well as say it out loud. The next person supplies the second sentence using another vocabulary word. This sentence is written after the first one as well as verbalized. Continue around the group until all the words are used. You can adapt the word form to fit your story.

* Make a multiple choice test using the words in this chapter. Wait 24 hours and then take your test. You can go to www.easytestmaker.com to make your test.

* Locate newspaper or magazine articles or sentences that have at least six of the vocabulary words from this chapter. Try to determine the word meaning from context. Highlight the context clues. You can look for various forms of the word or words with the targeted word parts.

## Expanded Word Forms

Select the appropriate word form for each of the sentences.

hypothermia   hyperthermia   hyperactive   democrats   democratic   democrat
democracy   apathy   apathetic   pathology   anomaly   anomalous

1. When presidential elections are held in the United States, you have the _____ and the Republicans campaigning in every state. Because the United States is a _____ country, it is important for the people to know the issues that each candidate professes, whether he or she a _____ or a republican. In a _____ the government is "of the people, by the people, for the people."

2. _____ in the classroom is not acceptable. Each student should be interested and demonstrate the desire to learn. Lack of interest can translate to poor attitude and low grades in the class. Although many students think it is acceptable to be _____ they should have empathy for the professor and try to feel what he or she feels when they show no desire to do well in the class.

3. The _____ report showed a(n) _____ in the _____ child's blood work. The doctors weren't sure whether the _____ findings were due to an infection or just that the child was extremely active and got overheated and exhausted.

4. It was unusual when the news broadcasters reported on a water skier suffering from _____ in the Caribbean and a snow skier suffered from extreme _____ at the North Pole.

*Puzzle Fun*

**Directions:** Each hint in the crossword puzzle is either a synonym or an antonym of one of the vocabulary words in this chapter. If the word before the hint is *synonym,* – find the synonym of the hint from your word list. If the word before the hint is *antonym,* – find the antonym of the hint from your word list.

**Across**

3. synonym—government by people
7. antonym—weak
11. synonym—diagnosis
15. synonym—diorama
16. synonym—prototype
17. antonym—commoner
18. synonym—all-knowing

**Down**

1. synonym—remedy
2. synonym—gross exaggeration
4. synonym—heatstroke
5. synonym—disinterest
6. synonym—king or queen
8. synonym—bedlam
9. synonym—ranking
10. synonym—subnormal body temperature
12. antonym—order, rule
13. antonym—not present
14. synonym—assumption
16. synonym—aberration

# CHAPTER FOUR

# Words: An Accessory for Learning

*"The words! I collected them in all shapes and sizes and hung them like bangles in my mind."*

Hortense Calisher (1911–2009)

## CHAPTER OBJECTIVE

**Students will be able to identify and use words with the following common structural elements:**

Roots: lat

Prefixes: de-, cata-, inter-, intra-

Suffixes: -al, -ic, -ium

## CHAPTER OUTLINE

 **Memory Tip**   Test/Retest

 **Learning Strategy**   Context Clues Part II

### Part A
*Words to Learn*

| | |
|---|---|
| lateral | psychological |
| bilateral | physiological |
| unilateral | solarium |
| | terrarium |

*Structural Elements*

-al  adj's ending          lat

-ic, -ium

### Part B
*Words to Learn*

| | |
|---|---|
| detractor | intramural |
| demoralize | intrastate |
| decipher | catalyst |
| interval | catastrophe |
| interpersonal | |

*Structural Elements*

de-   cata-

inter-, intra-

*Power Words*

| | |
|---|---|
| ameliorate | opulent |
| fervent | |

33

## 💡 *Memory Tip*   Test/Retest

Repetition is one of the requirements for learning. It takes multiple exposures to information to get it solidly into your long-term memory and have it available for retrieval. One way you can accomplish this when learning vocabulary is to practice testing yourself on the information. When you study, don't just read the material over and over; instead read the word and remember the definition or use it in a sentence. Practice remembering the definitions and check them only if necessary while you complete the exercises in the book.

In the following chapters you will learn multiple study strategies you can use for the memory tip of Test/Retest. Remember that you can also adapt these strategies to any learning situation in any class.

## 🔍 *Learning Strategy*   Context Clues Part II

In Chapter Three, the context clues of synonyms, antonyms, and direct definition were discussed. More context clues are presented in this chapter. Students often miss the most frequently used context clues of punctuation marks and examples. Punctuation marks are road signs to understanding what is read. These road signs can also assist in defining unfamiliar words. For example, in the following sentences the use of punctuation will lead you to word meaning.

* Fred wondered whether the picnic food was **edible**, able to be eaten, since the food was setting out in the summer heat for over three hours. (commas)

* Laura **retained** (kept) her maiden name after her recent marriage. (parentheses)

* Was Madonna **candid**—honest—in his recent interview? (dashes)

Examples are frequently used as context clues because the author can relate an unfamiliar word with someone or something that is familiar to the reader. The context clue of examples is used frequently in college textbooks. Read the following sentences and locate the example for each word in bold print.

* Punxsutawney Phil is the **prognosticator** that everyone waits to see on February 2. The tradition is that he will predict whether we will have an early spring or six more weeks of winter. (From this example you can conclude that the meaning is "forecaster" or "someone who predicts.")

* I **rationalized** for three days about not studying for midterm exams. I told my roommate that I had to clean my room, call my grandmother, and anything else I could think of instead of studying. (From this example of *rationalized*, you can guess the word means "reasons" or "excuses.")

Some key words that point out example clues are *example, such as, especially, for instance, like, other, such, and one kind of.*

The use of context clues will expedite, or speed up, the reading and comprehension process. Look for context clues around unfamiliar words before you go to the dictionary for word meaning.

## Part A

💬 *WORDS TO LEARN—SEE AND SAY*   Use the pronunciation guide on the first page of this book to help you SAY each word.

1. lateral          lăt′ər-əl

2. bilateral        bī-lăt′ər-əl

3. unilateral       yoo′nə-lăt′ər-əl

4. psychological    sī′kə-lŏj′ĭ-kəl

5. physiological    fĭz′ē-ə-lŏj′ĭ-kəl

6. solarium         sō-lâr′ē-əm

7. terrarium        tə-râr′ē-əm

*STRUCTURAL ELEMENTS*   Look at the structural elements of each word. Use these elements to unlock the word's meaning.

| | |
|---|---|
| -al | relates to, pertains to → *adj , ending* |
| lat | side → |
| -ic | relates to |
| -ium | relates to, house of → *none edding* |

*CONTEXT CLUES*   Read the sentences. Use the words around the unfamiliar word to determine the word's meaning. Words in bold are the vocabulary words; words in italic are the context clues.

1. Strong **lateral** forces are exerted *sideways* on the race car driver who is traveling around a bend.

2. *Korea and Japan* had a **bilateral** agreement on trade policies that has been in effect for many decades.

3. Amanda's mom said that her decision about the family's summer vacation was a **unilateral** decision because she was *the only person* who researched the vacation options.

4. Sarah enjoyed her **psychological** studies because she wanted to learn more about the *science of the mind and behavior.*

5. The doctor examined the *patient's legs and hips* to determine whether there was a **physiological** cause for the severe weakness.

6. The new Magnum Hotel offers its guests a beautiful panoramic view as *they sit in the sun-drenched* **solarium** that overlooks the city.

7. Parker was interested in creating a **terrarium** to *hold his snails and other small insects* so that he could watch their daily movements.

*DICTIONARY*   Read the following definitions.

1. **lateral**   noun/adjective

   **Etymology:** lat (side) al (relates to)

   (noun) A lateral part, projection, or appendage

   (adjective) Relating to, or situated at or on, the side (NOTE: This word is most commonly used as an adjective, but you may find reference to it as a noun or verb.)

   Stroke victims many times will have **lateral** paralysis on *one side* of their body.

   **Synonyms:** sideward, flanking

   **Antonym:** centered

   **Vocabulary Tip:** You can make a lateral career move, which means that your compensation and responsibilities stay about the same. For example: His new job was a lateral move; it was not a promotion or demotion.

2. **bilateral**   adjective

   **Etymology:** bi (two) lat (side) al (relates to)

   Having or formed of two sides; two-sided

   The **bilateral** decision to cancel the senior prom was made after many hours of discussion and debate *between both the student government representative and the school principal.*

   **Synonyms:** reciprocal, two-sided

   **Antonyms:** multilateral, unilateral

3. **unilateral**   adjective

   **Etymology:** uni (one) lat (side) al (relates to)

   Of, on, relating to, involving, or affecting only one side

   In a dictatorship, all decisions are **unilateral**, made by just *one person.*

   **Synonym:** one-sided

   **Antonyms:** bilateral, many-sided, multilateral

4. **psychological**   adjective

   **Etymology:** psych (mind) olog (study of or science or) al (relates to or pertains to)

   Of, relating to, or arising from the mind or emotions

   The **psychological** effects of the drugs caused the elderly man to begin to *hallucinate* immediately after taking the medication; although he suffered *no physical problems,* his family was concerned and consulted the doctor immediately.

   **Synonym:** mental

   **Antonym:** physiological

5. **physiological**   adjective

   **Etymology:** physio (body) ic (relates to) al (relating to)

   Being in accord with or characteristic of the normal functioning of a living organism

   The students studied the **physiological** makeup of a *frog's body* using 3D imaging on the computer.

   **Synonym:** bodily

   **Antonym:** psychological

6. **solarium**   noun

   **Etymology:** solar (sun) ium (relates to, house of)

   A room, gallery, or glassed-in porch exposed to the sun

   John built a **solarium** on the east side of his house so it would *catch the morning sun.*

   **Synonym:** sun parlor

7. **terrarium**   noun

   **Etymology:** terra (earth, land) ium (relates to, house of)

   A small enclosure or closed container in which selected living plants and sometimes small animals are kept and observed

   The traditional sixth-grade science project was to construct a **terrarium** out of a two-liter bottle and *grow small plants.*

## *Practice Exercises*

### *MULTIPLE CHOICE*

1. Where would a quarterback throw a <u>lateral</u> pass?
   a. down the center of the field
   b. into the end zone
   c. toward the sidelines
   d. at the head coach

2. How many people do you need for a <u>bilateral</u> decision?
   a. one
   b. two

c. three

d. four

3. Which of the following statements indicates a <u>unilateral</u> decision?

   a. "It's my way or the highway."

   b. "Let's go together to pick out the new car."

   c. "We will call for a vote of the membership."

   d. "I will consult with your mother and tell you our decision."

4. You would want to sit in a <u>solarium</u> because

   a. you are too hot and want some shade

   b. you need dark surroundings in order to read your phone screen

   c. you are looking for a dark environment to nap

   d. you want to enjoy the sunshine

5. What would you find in a <u>terrarium</u> at the pet store?

   a. turtles

   b. rocks

   c. plants

   d. all of the above

6. Which of the following areas would be a <u>psychological</u> study?

   a. the changes in format of the government food guidelines

   b. regular milk versus soy milk

   c. why eating almonds and walnuts is healthy

   d. how to encourage people to make healthy food choices

7. You could have <u>physiological</u> discomfort in

   a. your mind

   b. your imagination

   c. your foot

   d. your dreams

*FILL IN THE BLANK*   Select the BEST word for each sentence. Use each word only once.

lateral      bilateral      unilateral      physiological   psychological   solarium      terrarium

1. The doctor saw a small tumor on the left _____ part of the patient's brain.

2. My second-grade teacher had a _____ in our classroom where she kept a live turtle all year.

3. Beth enjoyed her _____ studies because she was interested in why people behave the way they do.

4. One selling point in the new house was the view of the backyard from the spacious _____.

5. Joe and Jim formed a new company to distribute their computer game. Whenever a decision needed to be made, they decided it would be a(n) _____ decision made by both of them.

6. Sally enjoyed her _____ studies because she was interested in how the body fights diseases.

7. All discussion ended when Billy's mother declared that his bedtime was a(n) _____ decision.

*CORRECT OR INCORRECT?*   If the sentence is correct, write a "C" on the line provided. If not, write an "I" for incorrect, then REWRITE the sentence to make it correct. You can change any part of a sentence to make it correct.

1. The doctor diagnosed the pain as <u>physiological</u> because it was imagined by the patient.

_____

2. I enjoy sitting in the <u>solarium</u> during the winter months when it is warmed by the afternoon sun.

   C _____

3. After he caught the pass, the football receiver moved <u>laterally</u> when he ran straight ahead down the center of the field.

   I _____ to the sideline _____

4. Sam's project for the science fair was a <u>terrarium</u> filled with plants from his backyard and also his pet lizard.

   C _____

5. The monarchy made a <u>bilateral</u> decision and declared war on the neighboring country.

   I _____ unlateral _____

6. After a vote of the membership, it was <u>unilaterally</u> decided that the meeting date would be moved from the 25th to the 26th.

   I _____

7. The doctor diagnosed Dale's problem as <u>psychological</u> because he had problems with his muscle and bone structure.

   I _____ Physiological _____

*SHORT ANSWER*   Write your answers on a separate sheet of paper.

1. If a crab moved <u>laterally</u>, how would it be moving? Draw you answer in picture form.
2. Describe a decision in your life that would be made <u>bilaterally</u>. Who would make the decision?
3. Describe a decision in your life that would be made <u>unilaterally</u>. Who would make the decision?
4. What would be some positive reasons to add a <u>solarium</u> to your current home?
5. What are three words that contain the structural element *terra?* These can be real or nonsense words.
6. Describe a <u>psychological</u> problem that would interfere with your performance on an exam.
7. Name two examples of a <u>physiological</u> injury.

# Part B

 **WORDS TO LEARN—SEE AND SAY**   Use the pronunciation guide on the first page of this book to help you SAY each word.

1. detractor        dĭ-trăkt-or
2. demoralize       dĭ-môr′ə-līz′
3. decipher         dĭ-sī′fer
4. interval         ĭn′tər-vəl
5. interpersonal    ĭn′tər-pûr′sə-nəl
6. intramural       ĭn′trə-myŏŏr′əl
7. intrastate       ĭn′trə-stāt′
8. catalyst         kăt′l-ĭst
9. catastrophe      kə-tăs′trə-fē

*STRUCTURAL ELEMENTS*   Look at the structural elements of each word. Use these elements to unlock the word's meaning.

| | |
|---|---|
| de- | down, apart, away from, reversal |
| cata- | down |
| inter- | between |
| intra- | within |

 *CONTEXT CLUES*   Read the sentences. Use the words around the unfamiliar word to determine the word's meaning. Words in bold are the vocabulary words; words in italic are the context clues.

1. The governor's **detractors** claim that his fierce temper *makes him undesirable* as a potential presidential candidate in the upcoming election.

2. The student was **demoralized** when he received a failing grade on the first exam; he *quit school* and *gave up his dream* of a college education.

3. The primary concern for first-grade students is to learn to **decipher** *what print means* in their reading books.

4. The twins saw each other at regular **intervals**—*usually once a month.*

5. Harmonious **interpersonal** relationships are very important in creating a good working environment *among coworkers.*

6. All the *sororities at the college played in* an **intramural** volleyball tournament to benefit their college's building fund.

7. The Ohio Electric Company's **intrastate** license enabled it to provide power only to the residents *within the state.*

8. Joe's failing grades at midterm were the **catalyst** that *caused* him to withdraw from college.

9. The 9/11 **catastrophe** *resulted in the deaths of thousands of people.*

 *DICTIONARY*   Read the following definitions.

1. detractor   noun

    **Etymology:** de (down, apart, away) tract (pull) or (something or someone)

    Something or someone that speaks ill of; someone who criticizes someone unfairly

    The acrobat's accident while performing was certainly a **detractor** *from the festivities* of the occasion.

    **Synonyms:** blamer, maligner

    **Antonym:** supporter

2. demoralize   verb

    **Etymology:** de (down, apart, away) moral (relating to character or will) ize (to make or cause to be)

    To undermine confidence or morale; dishearten

    The team was **demoralized** *after its fifth consecutive loss.*

    **Synonyms:** discourage, weaken

    **Antonym:** boost

3. **decipher**   verb

**Etymology:** de (down) cipher (understand)

To read or interpret ambiguous, obscure, or illegible matter; to convert from a code or cipher to plain text

The spy had to **decipher** *the coded messages* received from headquarters.

**Synonyms:** analyze, construe

4. **interval**   noun

**Etymology:** inter (between) vallum (wall) al (relates to)

A space between two objects, points, or units

Florida experiences many afternoon showers that have very short **intervals** between them. *The time between showers is usually filled with sunshine and heat.*

**Synonyms:** space, gap, intermission

**Antonym:** continuation

**Vocabulary Tip:** An *interval* is a gap of time or space, whereas an *interlude* (literally "between games") generally functions to fill such a gap, thus occupy an interval.

5. **interpersonal**   adjective

**Etymology:** inter (between) person (people) al (relates to)

Of or relating to the interactions between individuals

Excellent **interpersonal** skills were at the top of the job description for the director of human resources because so much of the job involved *working with the employees* in the company.

6. **intramural**   adjective

**Etymology:** intra (within) mural (walls) al (relates to or pertains to)

Existing or carried on within the bounds of an institution, especially a school

Megan signed up to participate in the newly formed **intramural** vollyball team because she thought it would be fun to *play against her classmates.*

**Synonym:** internal

**Antonym:** intercollegiate

7. **intrastate**   adjective

**Etymology:** intra (within) state (state)

Relating to or existing within the boundaries of the state

Since Ryan and Stephanie's recent move to Pennsylvania, they got lost when trying to find their way from Harrisburg to Pittsburgh because they were following the interstate highway when they should have been following the **intrastate** numbers that would guide them *within the state* instead of the highways that went between states.

**Synonym:** statebound

**Antonym:** interstate

8. **catalyst**   noun

**Etymology:** cata (down) lyst (derived or translated to mean loosen)

Someone or something that causes something to happen or change

The **catalyst** that *resulted in* Erin enrolling in college was not being able to find a good-paying job with benefits without a college degree.

**Synonyms:** stimulus, motivation

**Antonym:** damper

9. catastrophe   noun   *Big bad thing happen*

**Etymology:** cata (down) strophe (turn)

A great, often sudden calamity; a complete failure

Hurricane Katrina was a natural **catastrophe** from which people who live in New Orleans are still *trying to recover*.

**Synonym:** fiasco

**Antonym:** benefit

**Vocabulary Tip:** *Catastrophe* is a negative word (*cata* means down—something that brought down to the worst level) whereas *catalyst* is a neutral word (again *cata* means down—this time something broken down or turned down to cause something else to result were).

## Practice Exercises

### MULTIPLE CHOICE

1. Why would someone be a war <u>detractor</u>?
   a. He or she is completely behind the government's decisions.
   b. He or she does not believe in war.
   c. He or she owns a defense contract and anticipates making more money.
   d. He or she does not like to be part of controversy.

2. A child might be <u>demoralized</u> if he or she
   a. were never picked to play any games
   b. won all the games played in school
   c. had a sister who let him or her win at board games
   d. was on a championship debate team

3. On the submarine, the person in charge of <u>deciphering</u> the code would
   a. track all the boats in the area
   b. constantly watch the sonar screen
   c. transcribe the messages sent to the submarine
   d. make sure all the other seamen did their assigned jobs

4. In the <u>interval</u> between fall semester and spring semester, you could
   a. study with your roommate
   b. go to all your classes
   c. be elected president of your campus organization
   d. travel

5. Which phrase would encourage <u>interpersonal</u> communication?
   a. "What do you think?"
   b. "Let's just do what I want."
   c. "Don't say another word."
   d. "Do as I say, not as I do."

6. Which of the following would be competitors in <u>intramural</u> sports?
   a. two high schools in the state
   b. two teams of ninth-grade boys
   c. two parents and their preschool children
   d. faculty from the community college versus faculty from the university

7. Which of the following is an example of <u>intrastate</u>?
   - a. one country to another
   - b. United States to Canada
   - c. Ohio to Pennsylvania
   - d. New York City to Buffalo, New York

8. Which of the following might cause a <u>catastrophe</u>?
   - a. inheriting a lot of money
   - b. moving from one town to another
   - c. earning a poor grade on a college exam
   - d. a tornado

9. The <u>catalyst</u> for change in a company could be
   - a. the current president got a raise
   - b. a board of trustees who are satisfied with the profits
   - c. recent good reviews by the financial community
   - d. a new CEO

*FILL IN THE BLANK*  Select the BEST word for each sentence. Use each word only once.

detractors (7)   decipher (1)   demoralize (2)   interval (5)   interpersonal (3)
intramural (4)   intrastate (6)   catalyst (9)   catastrophe (8)

1. The spy was able to successfully _decipher_ the code and understand what the enemy was telling the troops.
2. You should be careful that you do not let one poor grade _demoralize_ you and discourage your efforts to complete your education.
3. It is important for doctors to have good _interpersonal_ skills so that they can communicate well with their patients.
4. Joe and Tom did not play on the school-sponsored basketball team, but they did like playing on the _intramural_ team.
5. The _interval_ between semesters gives both students and faculty a break from their academic work.
6. I signed up for the _intrastate_ do-not-call list; now I need to register for the national list.
7. Everyone approved of the new law except for a group of _detractors_ who looked at only the negative aspects.
8. After the _catastrophe_ the Red Cross helped families who had lost their homes.
9. The chemical _catalyst_ helped the other parts of the mixture complete the reaction as the chemist intended.

*CORRECT OR INCORRECT?*   If the sentence is correct, write a "C" on the line provided. If not, write an "I" for incorrect, then REWRITE the sentence to make it correct. You can change any part of a sentence to make it correct.

1. The <u>detractors</u> were so impressed with the skills of the new quarterback that they renewed his contract for another five years and gave him a bonus.

   I _____ not _____

2. The distraught student worked on his <u>interpersonal</u> peace by journaling and spending time in quiet contemplation.

   I _____ skills by spending time with others _____

3. In the movie *Windtalkers*, the Navajo Indians used a "code" that the enemy could not <u>decipher</u>.

   C _____

4. The <u>intramural</u> sports team competed against the other schools in the state.

   I _____

5. The <u>intrastate</u> truck driver was licensed to deliver goods only within his state.

C _____

6. The student who always earned Cs was <u>demoralized</u> when she earned an A on her physics exam.

I _____ A's _____

7. When practicing spaced learning, the <u>interval</u> between study periods is important to successful long-term retention.

C _____

8. ~~Everyone~~ felt refreshed and safe after the <u>catastrophe</u>.

I or No one _____

9. When the <u>catalyst</u> was added to the solution, the color changed.

C _____

*SHORT ANSWER*   Write your answers on a separate sheet of paper.

1. What would someone do if he or she were a <u>detractor</u> in a debate about the war?

2. List three <u>interpersonal</u> skills that you consider essential when living with roommates.

3. How is using word elements helpful when you have to <u>decipher</u> new words?

4. Name three things that have <u>intervals</u> between them. For example, in a play the intermission would be an <u>interval</u> between the acts.

5. If you participate in <u>intramural</u> sports, who are your opponents?

6. Name an event that might <u>demoralize</u> a student who is struggling to pass a course.

7. What state do you live in? If you drove <u>intrastate</u>, where could you go?

8. If a child were the <u>catalyst</u> in a playground fight, what might she have done?

9. What would be some environmental concerns after a <u>catastrophe</u> such as a flood?

# Power Words

1. **ameliorate**   ə-mēl′yə-rāt′   verb

   To make or become better; improve

   The teacher tried to **ameliorate** the discussion about Kara's repeating first grade so that her parents would not be upset and would *see the value* in the decision.

   **Synonym:** improve

   **Antonym:** harm

   **Vocabulary Tip:** Ameliorate is related to *alleviate* and *mitigate*, but is different in that it is specific to making something better. The other words mean easing or lessening something. Ameliorate is used to describe improving something that really needs improving.

2. **fervent**   fûr′-vənt   adjective

   Feeling with passion

   The **fervent** suitor *showered his intended* with flowers and candy *every day*.

   **Synonyms:** ardent, earnest

   **Antonyms:** dispirited, unenthusiastic

3. **opulent**   ŏp′yə-lənt   adjective

Rich, lavish

The king lived in an **opulent** castle. Everything was *gold plated or covered in silk.*

**Synonyms:** extravagant, showy

**Antonym:** meager

**Vocabulary Tip:** Although not always, many times *opulent* is used to describe lavish, expensive possessions that cast a negative light on their owner.

## Practice Exercises

1. Describe a situation that could be <u>ameliorated</u> with an inheritance of a million dollars.

2. What is something that you feel <u>fervent</u> about? Explain your answer.

3. If you could redecorate your home and make it <u>opulent</u>, what three things would you buy or change first?

# Chapter Review

## Extend Your Learning

Do one or more of the following exercises to practice the words in this chapter. Remember that it is important to use a variety of strategies in order to maximize your learning.

- Read your vocabulary words and their definitions into a voice recorder. Space your learning of the words throughout the week. Review the recorded lessons at least once a day. After five days, write and say each word and definition, then add a sentence using your understanding of the word. Read and record the sentences.

- Create a concept map of the words that are connected by their common word parts. Then add more words that you know or come across that have that same structural element.

- Using the vocabulary words from this chapter, write new sentences with clear context clues, or write a story using as many words as possible.

- For this activity you will need to have computer access. Go to www.easytestmaker.com or a similar site. At this site you will be able to create an objective quiz that you could take as a review exercise. You will have to register for the site, but you will not receive any spam or unsolicited emails. Once you log in, click on "Create a New Test." Use the words from this chapter to create a quiz with the following: multiple choice (five questions), true and false (ten questions), and fill in the-blank (five questions). Be prepared to take the quiz yourself and also to share the quiz with another student. You can use this site for creating any review quiz that you may need.

## Expanded Word Forms

Select the appropriate word form for each of the sentences.
demoralize ②   demoralizing ①   demoralized ①   catastrophe ④
catastrophic   decipher ③   deciphered ③   deciphering ③

1. Angelina was _____ *ecl* _____ when her friend told everyone that she wasn't able to pass the admissions requirements to get into the school of education. The _____ *ing* _____ statements caused Angelina to drop out of school.

2. It is very easy to _____ a young child, so it is the parents' responsibility to make sure that they find some praiseworthy comments to make before addressing any shortcoming a child may have.

3. During WWII, Joe's assignment was to _____ *er* _____ the enemy's coded messages. When he was _____ *ing* _____ the messages, he needed to work in an isolated, quiet place. One important message Joe _____ *ecl* _____ was about the enemy's plans to contaminate the water supply.

4. Jason was two years old, so when he lost his favorite blanket it was a _____ *phe* _____. The _____ *-phic* _____ event kept both Jason and his parents awake all night.

*Puzzle Fun*

**Across**
3. relating to the body
7. to dishearten
8. a small enclosure used for plants or small animals typically inside of a house or room
10. space between
11. gallery or room exposed to the sun
13. relating to a side
15. fiasco
17. make less severe
19. passionate

**Down**
1. relating to the mind
2. rich and lavish
4. relating to communication forms between people
5. two sided
6. one sided
9. agent of change
12. to break the code or to interpret
14. someone who criticizes someone unfairly
16. within the bounds of an institution
18. within the bounds of a state

# CHAPTER FIVE
# Headed in the Right Direction

*If you are headed in the right direction, each step,*
*no matter how small, is getting you closer to your goal.*

Anonymous

## CHAPTER OBJECTIVE

**Students will be able to identify and use words with the following common structural elements:**

Prefixes: em-, en-, ex-, e-, ec-, im-, in-
Suffixes: -ize , -tive, -ate

## CHAPTER OUTLINE

 **Memory Tip**   Overlearn the Material

 **Learning Strategy**   Primary Rehearsal Strategies

| Part A | | Part B | |
|---|---|---|---|
| *Words to Learn* | | *Words to Learn* | |
| connotative | denotative | embezzle | entrench |
| perspective | deceptive | eccentric | exhilarate |
| rationalize | abbreviate | empathy | insidious |
| infiltrate | | exonerate | impending |
| | | emigrate | |

*Structural Elements*

-ize, -tive

-ate

*Structural Elements*

em-, en-     ex-, e-, ec-
im-, in-

*Power Words*

mandatory

emulate

pervasive

extenuate

💡 *Memory Tip*    Overlearn the Material

Repeated review is necessary to advance to the overlearning stage. Once the material is overlearned, on-demand recall is improved. The goal of overlearning is to successfully file the information in your long-term memory.

🔍 *Learning Strategy*    Primary Rehearsal Strategies: Tri-Fold

Intending to remember (Chapter One) sounds incredibly easy, but it is important to develop strategies to help you do it. Remembering can be a challenge. It is crucial to find several strategies that will help increase the amount of information that can be remembered. With the tri-fold strategy, you are exposed to the material six times. Also by using the tri-fold you are addressing the seven steps to a powerful memory that was introduced in chapter one. This repetition and organization will help you store the information in your long-term memory. Give it a try! It really works!

## *Tri-Fold: Directions*

1. Take a sheet of paper and fold it lengthwise into three columns.

2. Label the three columns on the front A, B, and C.

3. Label the three columns on the back D, E, and F.

4. Write the words from Part A in column A.

5. Try to remember the definitions for the words in column A. Write as many definitions as you can in column B. Do not use your notes or textbook. If you don't know or are unsure of a definition simply draw a line in column B to help you to focus on the troublesome definition. Always go back and review any definition that is underlined.

6. Check your column B definitions with the textbook. Make any corrections or insert any definitions that you did not remember.

7. Fold back column A so that only columns B and C are showing. In column C, write the word for the definition that is in column B. When you are done, check column C with column A.

8. Repeat the process until all columns are filled.

Here is what you are doing to help yourself learn the information:

• Intend to remember: You have made a conscious decision to learn by being actively involved with the material.

• Organize the material: Limit the amount of information you put on each tri-fold column to seven (plus or minus two) items.

• Test/retest or repetition: After going through the tri-fold method you will have practiced the words a minimum of six times. This puts you well on your way to the next step.

• Overlearn the material: Continue to review the words even after you feel you know them.

• Use memory techniques: When using the tri-fold method, if you visualize, make an association, or use a mnemonic device, you increase the number of words you will remember.

• Space your learning over several study sessions: Either take a break between some of the folds or do the back of the tri-fold the next day. Your recall will improve if you space your learning over several study sessions.

• Study before bed: The tri-fold method is an easy one-page review that can be done or reviewed before bed to increase retention.

# Part A

🔊 *WORDS TO LEARN—SEE AND SAY*    Use the pronunciation guide on the first page of this book to help you SAY each word.

1. connotative          kŏn′ə-tā′-tǐv

2. perspective          pər-spĕk′tǐv

3. rationalize          răsh′ə-nə-līz′

4. denotative          dĭ-nō′tə-tĭv        *ize = verb*

5. denote              di-′nōt              *952 200 78 11*

5. infiltrate          ĭn-fĭl′trāt′

6. deceptive           dĭ-sĕp′tĭv

7. abbreviate          ə-brē′vē-āt′

 **STRUCTURAL ELEMENTS**   Look at the structural elements of each word. Use these elements to unlock the word's meaning.

-ize, -tive,          pertaining to; or to make        *ize → verb*

-ate                  to make or cause to be           *tive ⟹ adj*
                                                       *ate = verb*

 **CONTEXT CLUES**   Read the sentences. Use the words around the unfamiliar word to determine the word's meaning. Words in bold are the vocabulary words; words in italic are the context clues.

1. The **connotative** *feeling* of the color red usually suggests *warmth and passion.*

2. Because of her heritage and background, she has a unique **perspective**, *or viewpoint,* on the problems of her country.

3. Justin **rationalized** missing class *by saying* that he knew the information being presented and he could do the work on his own.

4. The covert mission was so successful that no one knew the agents had **infiltrated** the enemy headquarters and were *secretly working there* on a daily basis.

5. *The dictionary meaning*, or **denotative** meaning, of words is the most reliable.

6. She *did not tell us the truth*, but made **deceptive** remarks about the property to persuade us to buy it.

7. Joey's speech was so long that he had to **abbreviate**, *or shorten*, the introduction in order to have it fit into his assigned time on the program.

 **DICTIONARY**   Read the following definitions.

1. **connotative**   adjective

   Having the power of implying or suggesting something in addition to what is directly stated

   The **connotative** meaning for the word *flirt* is *negative*, just as the **connotative** meaning for the word *frugal* is more *positive*. It is very important to understand the *implied meaning* in order to completely understand what someone means.

   **Synonym:** inferential

   **Antonym:** explicit

2. **perspective**   noun

   **Etymology:** per (for each) spec (see or view) tive (act, state, or condition of)

   A mental view or outlook

   The *employees viewed* the prospect of a layoff from a different **perspective** *than management.*

   **Synonym:** awareness

3. **rationalize**   verb

   **Etymology:** ration (explanations, reasons) al (relates or pertains to) ize (to make or cause to be)

   To provide an explanation or reason for something; to devise self-satisfying but incorrect reasons for one's behavior

Sue *used her recent illness* to **rationalize** her failing grade on the exam.

**Synonyms:** excuse, reason, justify

**Antonyms:** complicate, puzzle

4. **infiltrate**   verb

**Etymology:** in (into) filt (filter) ate (to make or cause to be)

To pass (troops, for example) secretly into enemy-held territory; to cause (a liquid, for example) to permate a substance by passing through its pores; to become a member of a group or organization with the intent of gathering information or doing harm

The movie producer **infiltrated** *the secret society* and exposed all its secrets in a controversial documentary.

**Synonyms:** move in, penetrate

**Antonyms:** shield, stop

**Vocabulary Tip:** 'infiltrate' usually is used in reference to 'people' while 'percolate' is usually used when something is filtering through.

5. **denotative**   adjective

**Etymology:** de (down, apart, away) notate (noting, writing) tive (act, states, or condition of)

The most direct or specific meaning of a word.

Joe was careful to use the **denotative,** *or clearly understood,* meaning of words in his letter of resignation.

**denote**   verb

To mark or indicate; to refer to specifically.

The teacher used colored labels to **denote** *which group* of children went to lunch first.

**Synonym:** direct

**Antonym:** implied

**Memory Tip:** To keep the meanings of *connotative* and *denotative* straight, remember that both **d**ictionary and **d**enotative begin with the letter *D* and both are the literal meaning of a word.

6. **deceptive**   adjective

**Etymology:** de (down, apart, away from) cept (take) tive (act, state, or condition of)

Hiding the truth in order to get an advantage

The mother was **deceptive,** by *telling her child "maybe" when she really meant "no."*

**Synonym:** misleading

**Antonym:** truthful

7. **abbreviate**   verb

**Etymology:** abbrev (shorten) ate (to make or cause to be)

To make shorter; to reduce

It is important not to **abbreviate** the manual too much so that it doesn't become *so short* that your reader doesn't understand what steps are necessary.

**Synonyms:** abridge, condense

**Antonyms:** expand, lengthen

*Practice Exercises*

*MULTIPLE CHOICE*

1. When would it be appropriate to use the <u>connotative</u> meaning of a word?
   a. when writing a term paper
   b. when talking with your friends in the dorm
   c. when describing an accident to a police officer
   d. when applying for a school loan

2. When you examine situations from different <u>perspectives</u> you
   a. walk around outside for a while
   b. try to imagine how someone else might feel
   c. draw lines to see where they converge
   d. write about the situation step by step

3. A student who failed an exam might <u>rationalize</u> his or her grade by thinking
   a. my roommate skipped several classes
   b. the other students in the class got better grades
   c. the exam was unfair
   d. the professor provided the class with a study guide

4. Which of the following would someone want to <u>infiltrate</u>?
   a. coffee
   b. enemy troops
   c. drinking water filled with sediment
   d. cigarettes

5. Why is it important to use the <u>denotative</u> meaning of words when you are writing a term paper?
   a. They are easier to spell.
   b. It will make your paper more descriptive and interesting.
   c. It will help the reader know exactly what you mean.
   d. The editing will be faster.

6. Which of the following needs to be <u>deceptive</u>?
   a. a chef
   b. an undercover police officer
   c. a tax accountant
   d. the CEO of a major company

7. Which of the following is an example of an <u>abbreviated</u> word?
   a. *can't* for cannot
   b. *envir* for environment
   c. *I will* for I shall
   d. *maybe* instead of no

*FILL IN THE BLANK*    Select the BEST word for each sentence. Use each word only once.

connotative ⑤    perspective ⑥    rationalize ②    deceptive ①
denotative ④    infiltrate ③    abbreviated ⑦

1. The fraudulent accountant was __deceptive__ in his dealings with the stockholders of the company.
2. Many criminals __rationalize__ their actions by blaming events that occurred in their childhood.

3. One way rivals try to gain information is to have spies _infiltrate_ the opposing camp. They act like regular members, but are trying to locate secret information without being detected.

4. In order to be understood, you should speak carefully and know the _denotative_ meaning of a word as well as the connotative meaning.

5. Sue was not thinking of the _connotative_ meaning of the word when she referred to her friend as a "flirt."

6. You might have a different _perspective_ of an argument if you looked at it from your opponent's point of view.

7. Because of the bad weather, Professor Jones got to class late and had to deliver an _abbreviate_ version of his lecture instead of the entire lesson.

*CORRECT OR INCORRECT?*   If the sentence is correct, write a "C" on the line provided. If not, write an "I" for incorrect, then REWRITE the sentence to make it correct. You can change any part of the sentence to make it correct.

1. The <u>connotative</u> meaning of the word *skinny* is exactly the same as the meaning of the word *thin*.

   I _____

2. If you read your term paper from the <u>perspective</u> of your professor, you may be able see how you can improve it and earn a higher grade.

   C _____

3. The child tried to <u>rationalize</u> his behavior when he clearly told his mother that he had stolen candy from the store because he wanted it.

   I _____ not ___

4. In order to maintain the secrecy of the group's meeting place, they made it quite easy to <u>infiltrate</u> their membership.

   I _____

5. The dictionary provides the most common <u>denotative</u> meaning of words.

   C _____

6. You are communicating in a <u>deceptive</u> manner when you clearly state your goals and intended outcomes of a project.

   I _____

7. I love going to the ocean, so I was happy when my vacation was <u>abbreviated</u> and I got to stay an extra three days.

   I  I do not like going to the ocean _____ not ___

*SHORT ANSWER*   Write your answers on a separate sheet of paper.

1. Explain the meaning of the following adjectives. For each, give both a <u>connotative</u> and <u>denotative</u> meaning.

   cheap _____     _____

   frugal _____     _____

   skinny _____     _____

   thin _____     _____

2. Following homecoming weekend, a student failed a Monday morning exam. Describe both the professor's and the student's <u>perspective</u> of the situation.

3. How could you <u>rationalize</u> spending all of your paycheck on a weekend trip to the shore?

4. How could you start to <u>infiltrate</u> an opposing sports team on a rival campus?

5. Describe how a repairman might be <u>deceptive</u> when trying to get a homeowner to spend more money on repairs.

6. What is one class you would like to have <u>abbreviated</u>? What is one class you would like to have lengthened?

# Part B

 ***WORDS TO LEARN—SEE AND SAY***   Use the pronunciation guide on the first page of this book to help you SAY each word.

1. embezzle          ĕm-bĕz′əl
2. eccentric         ĭk-sĕn′trĭk, ĕk-
3. empathy           ĕm′pə-thē
4. exonerate         ĭg-zŏn′ə-rāt′
5. emigrate          ĕm′ĭ-grāt′
6. entrench          ĕn-trĕnch′
7. exhilarate        ĭg-zĭl′ə-rāt′
8. insidious         ĭn-sĭd′ē-əs
9. impending         ĭm′-pĕnd-ing          *My right Oil*

 ***STRUCTURAL ELEMENTS***   Look at the structural elements of each word. Use these elements to unlock the word's meaning.

| | |
|---|---|
| em-, en- | put into |
| ex-, e-, ec- | out, away |
| im-, in- | ~~not~~ *into* |

***CONTEXT CLUES***   Read the sentences. Use the words around the unfamiliar word to determine the word's meaning. Words in bold are the vocabulary words; words in italic are the context clues.

1. He **embezzled** *company funds* to pay for his vacation in Europe.

2. The driver of the car was acting so **eccentric**, or *strange*, that the police thought he might be ill.

3. I have **empathy** for you in your fear about speaking to a group. *I felt the same way* before I took a public speaking class.

4. The report **exonerated** the crew *from all responsibility* for the collision.

5. The Cuban **emigration** *to the United States* caused the government much concern.

6. The weeds were so **entrenched** in the garden that they completely *took all the ground nutrients* from the plants.

7. Many runners feel **exhilarated** and *energetic* after a race.

8. Increased drug use was an **insidious** problem that *had a stronghold* on the high school *before anyone realized it was happening*.

9. The *quickly gathering dark clouds on the horizon* were a sign of the **impending** storm.

*DICTIONARY*   Read the following definitions.

1. **embezzle**   verb

   **Etymology:** em (into) bezz (destroy)

   To secretly take money that is in one's care or that belongs to an organization or business for one's own use

   Joe **embezzled** money *from his company* in order to pay off his credit card bills by *keeping two sets of books.*

   **Synonyms:** filch, steal

2. **eccentric**   adjective/noun

   **Etymology:** ec (out) centr (center) ic (relating to or pertaining to)

   (adjective) Odd in behavior, departing from established norm or pattern

   The police thought Tommy was the criminal because his **eccentric** behavior *made him stick out* from the rest of the onlookers.

   (noun) One who departs from established norm or pattern

   Joe was such an **eccentric** that everyone expected him to *do odd things.*

   **Synonym:** bizarre

   **Antonyms:** normal, conventional

3. **empathy**   noun

   **Etymology:** em (into) pathy (feelings)

   The ability to share someone else's feelings or experiences by imagining what it would be like to be in his or her situation

   Because she had once been a struggling student, Dr. Smith had **empathy** *for her failing students* and gave them extra help.

   **Synonyms:** compassion, appreciation

4. **exonerate**   verb

   **Etymology:** ex (out) onus (burden, guilt) ate (to make or cause to be)

   To be free from blame or guilt

   When *someone else confessed* to the crime, the prisoner was **exonerated**.

   **Synonyms:** vindicate, discharge

   **Antonym:** accuse

5. **emigrate**   verb

   **Etymology:** e (out) migr (move) ate (to cause to be, to make)

   To leave one's country or region to settle in another

   After the Civil War, many former slaves **emigrated** *from the South to the North* where they were able to find work.

   **Synonym:** move

   **Memory Tip:** *Emigrate, immigrate,* and *migrate* are confused many times. Remember the following:

   • *Emigrate* is from the point of view of the departure. Think *exit.*

   • *Immigrate* is from the point of view of the destination. Think *come in.*

   • *Migrate* is all about the moving. Think *move.*

   (www.vocabulary-vocabulary.com)

6. **entrench**   verb

   **Etymology:** en (into) trench (trench)

   Establish in a strong position

   The bats were so **entrenched** in the house attic that the owners had to call in *an expert to have them removed.*

   **Synonyms:** establish, anchor

7. **exhilarate**   verb

   **Etymology:** ex (out) hilar (cheerful) ate (to make or cause to be)

   To cause to feel happily refreshed and energetic

   To many stunt men the sense of danger **exhilarates** them and they are addicted to the *rush of feeling.*

   **Synonyms:** elate, invigorate, stimulate

8. **insidious**   adjective

   **Etymology:** in (into) sider (sit) ious (full of or characteristic of)   ~ ous = adj

   Harmful and destructive in a slow and gradual way

   Cancer is an **insidious** disease that often *goes undetected* until it is too late.

   **Synonym:** cunning

   **Antonym:** innocuous

9. **impending**   adjective

   **Etymology:** im (into) pendere (hangover)

   About to happen or take place; possibly something threatening

   After the jury found the defendant guilty, he had to *wait for* his **impending** sentence.

   **Synonym:** imminent

   **Antonym:** unlikely

   **Memory Tip:** *Impending* and *imminent* are words that indicate something is going to happen soon. *Imminent* usually refers to something negative; *impending* is more neutral.

   **Vocabulary Tip:** Don't confuse *imminent* with its homophone (words that sound the same but mean something different and may be spelled differently) *eminent*, which means "important or of high standing."

## *Practice Exercises*

### *MULTIPLE CHOICE*

1. What is something that would be <u>embezzled</u>?
   a. grades
   b. money
   c. mile
   d. extra hours at work

2. Which of the following might *not* be considered <u>eccentric</u>?
   a. wearing a navy red sock and a black sock
   b. wearing one shoe and one sandal
   c. carrying an umbrella on a cloudy day
   d. talking to yourself while shopping for groceries

3. The statement "Don't judge someone until you have walked in his or her shoes" is an example of
   a. enhancement
   b. euphemism
   c. eulogy
   d. empathy

4. Which of the following is something that is *not* an example of an <u>entrenched</u> habit?
   a. a custom
   b. eating at the same restaurant every Thursday
   c. trying different flavors of ice cream
   d. always ordering vanilla ice cream

5. The most accurate example of <u>emigration</u> is
   a. moving from England to Germany
   b. moving into a new community
   c. working in a state different than your home state
   d. banking off-shore

6. Which of the following could be called "<u>insidious</u>"?
   a. planning a surprise birthday party
   b. planning a vacation
   c. planning when to go school shopping
   d. planning a hostile takeover of a company

7. Which of the following words would describe someone who felt <u>exhilarated</u>?
   a. Energized, thrilled
   b. Sad, depressed
   c. Morbidly funny
   d. Nervous, anxious

8. After the prisoner was <u>exonerated</u>
   a. he was released from jail and allowed to go home
   b. his sentence was doubled
   c. he was given kitchen duty for the next six months
   d. he was allowed to start spending afternoons in the jail law library

9. If you were worried about an <u>impending</u> hurricane, which of the following might you do?
   a. return home to assess the damages
   b. stock up on food and bottled water
   c. go to the movies and buy extra popcorn
   d. invite your old friends for a visit

*FILL IN THE BLANK*   Select the BEST word for each sentence. Use each word only once.

embezzling     emigrated     exonerated     empathy
eccentric      entrenched    exhilarated    insidious
impending

1. Carol had a hard time going to sleep because she felt so _exhilarated_ by the great reviews she received for her performance in the lead role in the school play.

2. Jack was so _exhilarated_ that he didn't notice when everyone looked at him with disbelief.

3. When you have _empathy_ for others, you try to understand how they are feeling.

4. The accountant was indicted for _embezzle_ money from the company.

5. To avoid persecution by the government, the family _emigrate_ from their home to a different country.

6. The _insidious_ weed took over the garden before the owner realized it was a problem.

7. After the police found the real criminal, the innocent man who was in jail was _Exonerated_

8. Jill was so firmly _entrenched_ in her daily routine that the slightest change of plans made her uncomfortable.

9. The _impending_ exam the next day made it hard for Jeremy to sleep the night before.

**CORRECT OR INCORRECT?**    If the sentence is correct, write a "C" on the line provided. If not, write an "I" for incorrect, then REWRITE the sentence to make it correct. You can change any part of the sentence to make it correct.

1. The accountant was very honest and followed the tax codes perfectly when he <u>embezzled</u> the company's money.

   _I_        _dishonest not follow_

2. The <u>eccentric</u> young artist expressed his style by wearing a suit and tie to the job interview.

   _I_

3. It was obvious that the employer had great <u>empathy</u> for her employees. She never listened to any excuses and did not allow anyone to miss work because of family problems.

   _I_

4. Once Ellie confessed to spilling the juice on the new carpet, J.J. was <u>exonerated</u> from blame.

   _C_

5. <u>Emigration</u> laws prohibit people from moving from one country to another without proper documentation.

   _I_

6. Sally felt <u>exhilarated</u> after her terrible experience of failing her driver's exam.

   _I_        _she passed her driver's exam._

7. Darlene was spontaneous and flexible; therefore, most of her daily activities were firmly <u>entrenched</u> in her habits.

   _I_        _not_

8. The <u>insidious</u> virus infected the entire school within one week.

   _C_

9. It was with a sense of <u>impending</u> doom that Nancy walked into the principal's office to meet about her son.

   _C_

**SHORT ANSWER**    Write your answers on a separate sheet of paper.

1. Describe how an accountant might <u>embezzle</u> money from a company.

2. How would an <u>eccentric</u> professor act in class?

3. Describe a situation in which you would want a professor to have <u>empathy</u>.

4. What activities or habits are <u>entrenched</u> in your lifestyle?

5. Write a sentence that contains a clear context clue for the word <u>emigrate</u>.

6. What is a fictitious, <u>insidious</u> rumor that could cause problems if it spread through your school?

7. What would be needed to <u>exonerate</u> a person convicted of robbing a bank?

8. List two things that make you feel <u>exhilarated</u>.

9. Have you ever felt a sense of <u>impending</u> doom? If so, when?

## Power Words

1. **mandatory**   măn′də-tôr′ē   adjective

   Required or commanded by authority; obligatory

   The **mandatory** meetings were part of the rehabilitation process that the criminal was *required to* complete in order to satisfy his probation.

   **Synonyms:** required, compulsory

   **Antonym:** optional

2. **emulate**   em-yə-′lāt   verb

   To strive to equal or excel, especially through imitation

   Eric tried to **emulate** his older brother's athletic skills so that he *would also get* an athletic scholarship.

   **Synonyms:** copy, equal

   **Vocabulary Tip:** Emulate does not mean the same as imitate—imitate means simply to copy whereas emulate means to strive to equal or exceed someone's success.

3. **pervasive**   pər-vā′əsĭv   adjective

   Spreading through everything

   The **pervasive** smell from the burnt popcorn was *in every room* of the dorm.

   **Synonyms:** permeating, prevalent

   **Antonym:** narrow, localized

4. **extenuate**   ik-′sten-yə-wāt   verb

   To lessen or attempt to lessen the seriousness of something, especially by providing partial excuses to lessen the force of an accusation

   The bank robber told the court that there were **extenuating** circumstances that should be *taken into consideration* before he was sentenced for his crime.

   **Synonym:** ameliorate

   **Antonyms:** accuse, blame

### *Practice Exercises*

1. What courses are <u>mandatory</u> at your college or university?

2. Who is someone you would like to <u>emulate</u>? Why?

3. Name two things that could become <u>pervasive</u> in an elementary school.

4. What excuses would <u>extenuate</u> the accident of breaking your aunt's favorite lamp?

## Chapter Review

### *Extend Your Learning*

Use one or more of the following exercises to practice the words in this chapter. Remember that it is important to use a variety of strategies in order to maximize your learning.

- Using different-color pens or pencils, write the vocabulary word with its definition in one color. Use a different color for each word and definition. Continue down the page until you have written all the words and definitions. When you are taking the exam, visualize your work with the different colors.

- Say the vocabulary words out loud. Recite the definitions. Repeat this process several times throughout the week.

- Write a sentence for each of the vocabulary words. Use context clues in the sentence to indicate your understanding.

- Write the words on study cards (words on front and definitions on back, one word per card). Go through each card, look at the word, and recite the definition. Check your work. Separate the cards into two piles— the words that you know and the ones that you need to study. Repeat the ones you missed until you can recite them all correctly. Do the same thing tomorrow!

## Expanded Word Forms

Select the appropriate word form for each of the sentences.

exonerate        exonerated        exonerating        embezzling        embezzled        embezzler
deceptive        deceptively        deceived

1. Mark _____ told his girlfriend that he was working on a project in the library until after midnight when actually he was at a fraternity party off campus.

2. Ellen and Morgan were taught that being _____ was morally wrong; therefore, when they became friends with other girls at the university, it was very difficult to accept the way that they _____ others.

3. After four years in the state prison, Jim was _____ because of new evidence that was discovered.

4. To _____ a convicted criminal additional evidence must be provided.

5. After _____ the convicted embezzler, the job of the FBI is now to find the person who is responsible for the missing million dollars.

6. Joe was caught after he had _____ thousands of dollars from the business where he worked. The employer thought something was wrong because, while he was _____ the money Joe bought a new car and a new house. As a convicted _____ Joe was sentenced to five years in prison.

*Puzzle Fun*

**Directions:** For each clue in the puzzle, select a synonym from the words in this chapter. You can use the dictionary sections for help.

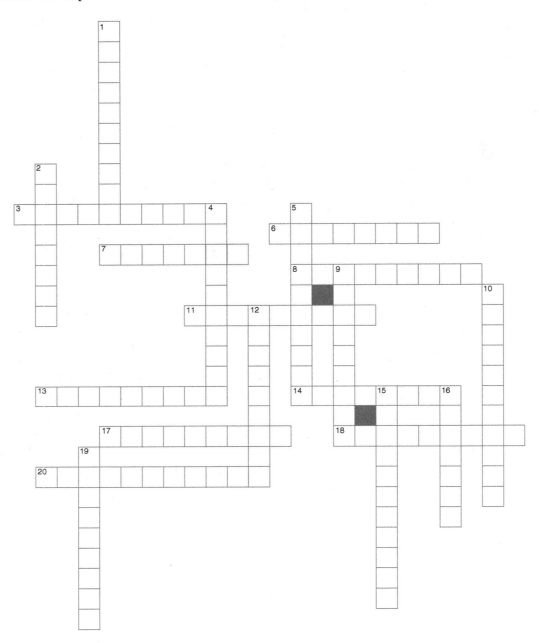

**Across**

3. verb/condense
6. verb/establish
7. noun/compassion
8. adjective/imminent
11. adjective/required
13. verb/vindicate
14. verb/move
17. adjective/bizarre
18. verb/ameliorate, lessen
20. adjective/inferential

**Down**

1. adjective/direct meaning
2. verb/steal
4. verb/invigorate
5. verb/penetrate
9. adjective/prevalent
10. noun/awareness
12. adjective/misleading
15. verb/justify
16. verb/copy
19. adjective/cunning

# CHAPTER SIX

## Constant Review:
## An Effective Strategy

*One forgets words as one forgets names. One's vocabulary needs constant fertilizing or it will die.*

Evelyn Waugh, English author (1903–1966)

---

## CHAPTER OBJECTIVE

**Students will be able to identify and use words with the following common structural elements:**

Roots: script, scribe, fer, nym, nom
Prefix: pseudo-

---

## CHAPTER OUTLINE

 **Memory Tip**   Space Your Learning

 **Learning Strategy**   Metacognition

### Part A
### *Words to Learn*

| | |
|---|---|
| deference | transfer |
| transcribe | confer |
| postscript | scribe |
| infer | |

### *Structural Elements*
script, scribe

fer

### Part B
### *Words to Learn*

| | |
|---|---|
| pseudoscience | synonym |
| pseudonym | antonym |
| nominate | nominal |
| anonymous | |

### *Structural Elements*

| | |
|---|---|
| pseudo- | nym, nom |

### *Power Words*

| | |
|---|---|
| empirical | albatross |
| imply | narcissism |

## 💡 *Memory Tip*  Space Your Learning

You improve your learning by dividing the task into meaningful "chunks" and by spacing your learning over several study periods. When doing this, try to organize the information so that you are working with seven bits of information at a time. Remember, the optimal number for remembering is seven, plus or minus two. (For more information, refer to Chapter One)

## 🔍 *Learning Strategy*  Metacognition

Metacognition is needed to be a successful student. It means that you (1) are aware of what you know, (2) are aware of what you don't know, and (3) develop a way of monitoring the success of new learning.

The Primary Rehearsal Strategy (PRS) tri-fold, explained in Chapter Five, is one way you can monitor your metacognitive abilities. Another such strategy is the use of concept cards (remember "flash cards" in elementary school?). This timeless strategy is used by many successful college students. You can adapt these strategies to any of your courses.

To make concept cards for your vocabulary, put the vocabulary word on the front of the index card and the definition and a sentence using the word on the back of the card. You can also add pronunciation, parts of speech, etc.

You should use a three-step process (identify the words that you know; identify the words that you don't know; and monitor new learning) when using concept cards. This process helps you to monitor your learning and learn the information by practicing test/retest.

- Go through the cards one at a time.

- Read the information on the front; try to recite the definition.

- Look back and check your recall.

As you go through the cards, separate the cards into three piles; those that you know, those you do not know, and those that you may know in part but not completely. (This is metacognition—being aware of what you know and don't know.) Continue to go through the ones that you do not know until you can get them all correct. And tomorrow? Do it again!

## Part A

🗫 *WORDS TO LEARN—SEE AND SAY*  Use the pronunciation guide on the first page of this book to help you SAY each word.

1. deference — dĕf′ər-əns

2. transcribe — trăn-skrīb′

3. postscript — pōst′skrĭpt′

4. infer — ĭn-fûr′ (verb),   inference  ĭn′fər-əns (noun)

5. confer — kən-fûr

6. scribe — skrīb

7. transfer — trăns-fur′

 *STRUCTURAL ELEMENTS*  Look at the structural elements of each word. Use these elements to unlock the word's meaning.

| | |
|---|---|
| script, scribe | write |
| fer | yield, bear |

*CONTEXT CLUES*   Read the sentences. Use the words around the unfamiliar word to determine the word's meaning. Words in bold are the vocabulary words; words in italic are the context clues.

1. In **deference** to our military personnel, we fly the American flag as our symbol of *respect for all of their courageous work.*

2. Taped recordings of witnesses' testimonies were **transcribed** *word for word* by clerk typists and entered into the court records.

3. As a **postscript** to the *story I told you last week, it turned out* that the unidentified woman was his sister-in-law.

4. I **inferred** *from Donna's expression* that she had doubts about what I was saying, even though she said that she agreed with me.

5. After earning my associate's degree from the community college, I plan to **transfer** my credits *to the state university* to earn my bachelor's degree in nursing.

6. After weeks of depositions and brainstorming meetings, the team of attorneys *met* to **confer** *about the best defense strategies* for the upcoming murder trial.

7. David was employed as a **scribe** in the Ancient Greek Department at the University. His job was to *write the English translation of an ancient Greek text.*

 *DICTIONARY*      Read the following definitions.

1. deference   noun

   **Etymology:** de (down, apart away) fer (yield or bear) ence (state, act, or condition of)

   Submission or courteous yielding to the opinion, wishes, or judgment of another

   The class was *honored* to have the esteemed forensic expert teach their class and *showed him* complete **deference** while he was lecturing.

   **Synonyms:** honor, respect

   **Antonym:** disrespect

2. transcribe   verb

   **Etymology:** trans (across) scribe (to write)

   To make a complete written record of spoken or written words

   The court stenographer **transcribed** the witness's testimony *so that it could be read later.*

   **Synonyms:** translate, record

3. postscript   noun

   **Etymology:** post (after) script (something written)

   A message added at the end of a story or letter

   There is a **postscript** to this story that tells *what happened three months later.*

   **Synonyms:** appendix, footnote

4. infer   verb  → the listener infer : The recover infer

   **Etymology:** in (into) fer (yield or bear)

   To reach an opinion from available information or facts

   Karen **inferred** *from her father's angry expression* that she and her date had stayed out too late.

inference   noun

An opinion reached by examining available information or facts

Most *people make the* **inference** *that I had been promoted because my father owned the company.*

**Synonyms:** (verb) deduce, derive (noun) deduction

💡 **Memory Tip:** Remember the following: The writer or speaker "implies" and the reader or listener "infers."

5. transfer   verb/noun

**Etymology:** trans (across) fer (yield)

(verb) Move or yield across from one place to another; to move

Brian had to **transfer** his bank account *from Ohio to Virginia* after his recent move.

(noun) The movement or ownership of right, title, or property from one person to another

*The* **transfer** *of the money was completed* after he signed all of the paperwork.

**Synonyms:** (verb) move, (noun) movement

**Antonym:** stay

6. confer   verb

**Etymology:** con (together or together with) fer (yield or bear)

To meet in order to deliberate together or compare ideas

The doctor **conferred** *with a specialist* before deciding on the treatment for his patient.

**Synonym:** consult

**Vocabulary Tip:** The word *confer* has a much stronger meaning that just to discuss. *Confer* denotes a more serious decision-making process.

7. scribe   noun

**Etymology:** scrib (write or written, someone who writes)

A professional copyist of manuscripts and documents

The author preferred to do her writing by hand on legal tablets. She employed two **scribes** *who entered all of her work into the computer for her.*

**Synonyms:** journalist, note taker

## *Practice Exercises*

### *MULTIPLE CHOICE*

1. Where would you expect to receive <u>deferential</u> treatment?
   a. in jail
   b. in the tax collector's office when paying your late taxes
   c. in an expensive hotel
   d. in the park while walking your dog

2. When the student <u>transcribed</u> his notes, he
   a. borrowed notes from a good student in the class
   b. rewrote his notes so they were clearer
   c. asked his professor for help with information that he did not understand
   d. compared notes with a classmate in his study group

3. Sue added a <u>postscript</u> to her letter because *After a little* *P. S.*
   a. she thought of something else she wanted to tell her friend
   b. she wanted her friend to know who the letter was from
   c. she wanted to be sure her friend knew the date it was written
   d. the letter was too long and she wanted to make it shorter

4. <u>Infer</u> means the same as
   a. deduce *or assume*
   b. make up
   c. complete
   d. investigate

5. If you <u>transferred</u> your belongings, what would you do?
   a. give them away
   b. move them from one place to another
   c. wash them
   d. share them with your roommate

6. It was important for Wanda and Wayne to <u>confer</u> before
   a. they decided to buy a new house
   b. Wanda went to the grocery store
   c. Wayne went bowling
   d. the grass needed to be mowed

7. When would you need someone to act as a <u>scribe</u> for you?
   a. if you broke your leg and had to move around on crutches
   b. if you are right-handed and broke your right hand
   c. if you needed information about how to complete an application for graduate school
   d. if you did not understand the French restaurant's menu

*(handwritten margin notes: reduce / Agine / deduce / take away / in cluee → to lead)*

*FILL IN THE BLANK*   Select the BEST word for each sentence. Use each word only once.

deference (4)   transcribe (3)   postscript (1)   infer (5)
transfer (2)    scribe (7)       conferred (6)

1. After she ended her letter, she thought of one more thing she wanted to say, so she added a _____.

2. Be careful when you *transcribe* money from your savings account to your checking account. Make certain that the account numbers are correct.

3. Karen's lecture notes were messy, so she had to _____ them so they were readable.

4. When you are speaking to a public official, it is polite to speak with _____, even if you do not agree with his opinion.

5. He could only _____ that his girlfriend wanted to break up with him by how she acted; she would not come right out and say the words.

6. The dean of students and the provost _____ about the Homecoming schedule for the parade and football game before they met with the student representatives.

7. When Jared hurt his hand playing football, he had to get a _____ to write his essay exams for him.

*CORRECT OR INCORRECT?*   If the sentence is correct, write a "C" on the line provided. If not, write an "I" for incorrect, then REWRITE the sentence to make it correct. You can change any part of the sentence to make it correct.

1. The salesperson <u>lost</u> a big sale because he <u>insulted</u> the customer with his <u>deference</u>.
   *I* _____ *get* _____ *respect* _____

2. After the secretary <u>transcribed</u> her meeting notes, she sent them to the attendees.

   _____

3. The author started her book with a <u>postscript</u> to introduce the reader to the characters and setting of the novel.

   _____

4. It was easy to study for the biology exam because Dr. Hill always <u>inferred</u> what was on the test.

   _____

5. Eric wanted to <u>transfer</u> twelve credits from the community college to the university.

   _____

6. Joe and Jenny broke up after they were able to amiably <u>confer</u> about the size of Jenny's engagement ring.

   _____

7. An early reading activity is for a young child to dictate a story and the teacher to be the <u>scribe</u> and write down the child's words.

   _____

*SHORT ANSWER*   Write your answers on a separate sheet of paper.

1. Would you like to receive <u>deferential</u> treatment at a restaurant? Why? Give one example of the type of treatment you would receive.

2. If you were asked to <u>transcribe</u> someone's lecture notes, what are you being asked to do? Why might this be a difficult assignment?

3. Why would you add a <u>postscript</u> to a letter you are writing?

4. Why is being able to <u>infer</u> information an important reading skill?

5. Describe two ways to <u>transfer</u> money from one account to another.

6. Explain how the verb <u>confer</u> is related to the noun <u>conference</u>.

7. What are two situations in which you might act as a <u>scribe</u> for another family member?

# Part B

*WORDS TO LEARN—SEE AND SAY*   Use the pronunciation guide on the first page of this book to help you SAY each word.

1. pseudoscience        sōō'dō-sī'əns

2. pseudonym            sōōd'n-ĭm'

3. nominate             nŏm'ə-nāt'

4. anonymous            ə-nŏn'ə-məs

5. synonym              sĭn'ə-nĭm'

6. antonym              ăn'tə-nĭm'

7. nominal              nŏm'ə-nəl

*STRUCTURAL ELEMENTS*    Look at the structural elements of each word. Use these elements to unlock the word's meaning.

pseudo-                     false

nym, nom                    name

 *CONTEXT CLUES*    Read the sentences. Use the words around the unfamiliar word to determine the word's meaning. Words in bold are the vocabulary words; words in italic are the context clues.

 1. Many scientists describe *astrology* as a **pseudoscience** *whereas the true science of astronomy* is recognized as a true science.

2. *Dr. Seuess* is a **pseudonym** for *Dr. Theodore Seuss Geisel* just like *Mark Twain* is a **pseudonym** for *Samuel Clemens.*

3. The president of the student government **nominated** his best friend *for the office of vice president.*

4. The FBI was actively *working to identify the author* of the threatening **anonymous** letter sent to the senator.

5. A **synonym** for *house* is *dwelling.*

6. The word *day* is the **antonym** for the word *night.*

7. The **nominal** fee for next-day delivery was *so small* that I had the package shipped that way.

 *DICTIONARY*    Read the following definitions.

1. **pseudoscience**   noun

   **Etymology:** pseudo (false) sci (knowledge) ence (state, act, or condition of)

   A theory, methodology, or practice that is considered to be without scientific foundation.

   I believe that the Ouiji Board can predict the future, but my mother says it is a *fake* and a **pseudoscience**.

   **Synonym:** false science

   **Antonym:** true science

2. **pseudonym**   noun

   **Etymology:** pseudo (false) nym (name)

   Fictious name

   Movie stars often make dinner reservations using a **pseudonym** because *they do not want the press to know* where they will be.

   **Synonym:** alias

3. **nominate**   verb

   **Etymology:** nom (name) ate (to make or cause to be)

   To propose by name as a candidate, especially for election; to designate or appoint to an office, responsibility, or honor

   Sam's teacher thought his short stories were written so well that she *nominated him for the senior class writing prize.*

   **Synonyms:** propose, suggest

   **Antonyms:** remove, dismiss

4. **anonymous**   adjective

   **Etymology:** an (not or without) nym (name) ous (full of or characteristic of)

   Having an unknown or unacknowledged name; having no distinctive character or recognition factor

   The people who offered to pay the rent for the homeless family wanted to remain **anonymous**; *their name would not be made public*, so that no one else would ask them for the same gift.

   **Synonyms:** nameless, unidentified

   **Antonyms:** identified, named

5. **synonym**   noun

   **Etymology:** syn (same) nym (name)

   A word having the same or nearly the same meaning as another word or words

   You should not use the same word several times in one sentence. Try to find a **synonym** that *means the same* to use instead.

   **Synonym:** same

   **Antonyms:** different, opposites

6. **antonym**   noun

   **Etymology:** ant (opposite or against) nym (name)

   A word meaning the opposite of another word

   *Day and night* are **antonyms**.

   **Synonym:** opposite

   **Antonyms:** synonym

7. **nominal**   adjective

   **Etymology:** nom (name) al (relates to or pertains to)

   Very small; in name only

   Because the *difference* between the two scores was so **nominal**, the contest was *declared a tie*.

   Sam was the **nominal** president of the organization, but all of the *decisions were made by the faculty sponsor*.

   **Synonyms:** insignificant, so-called

   **Antonyms:** significant, important

## *Practice Exercises*

### *MULTIPLE CHOICE*

1. For which would you be <u>nominated</u>?
   a. to leave for vacation a day early
   b. to be allowed to bring your dog to work
   c. to win a prize for the best short story
   d. to have a parking ticket fine forgiven

2. Words that are <u>synonyms</u>
   a. mean the opposite
   b. have slightly different meanings
   c. are spelled the same
   d. mean the same

3. Words that are <u>antonyms</u>
   a. mean the opposite
   b. have slightly different meanings
   c. are spelled the same
   d. mean the same

4. If someone wanted to be <u>anonymous</u>, he or she would
   a. make a grand entrance at a party
   b. not sign his or her name
   c. wear bright colors and lots of jewelry
   d. travel with several people who assist him or her

5. Why would a famous author use a <u>pseudonym</u> when writing a new book?
   a. because she doesn't want people to know that she had written it
   b. because she wants all the publicity that she can get
   c. because her first book was a huge success and she wants to build on that publicity
   d. because the second book is a sequel to the first

6. Which of the following do some people consider a <u>pseudoscience</u>?
   a. chemotherapy
   b. biology
   c. psychology
   d. reading tarot cards

7. The <u>nominal</u> leader of a group would
   a. make all of the decisions
   b. do all of the work
   c. decide whether his group would support a new local ordinance
   d. read a speech written by the real leader

*FILL IN THE BLANK*   Select the BEST word for each sentence. Use each word only once.

nominated①       synonyms⑤       antonyms⑥       anonymous②
pseudoscience④   pseudonym③      nominal⑦

1. I spoke at the meeting and _____ Joe to run for president of the organization.

2. David White, the famous actor, wanted his contribution to the charity to be _____, so he sent cash in an unmarked envelope.

3. Jeff was in protective custody, so he had to use a(n) _____ when getting a new driver's license.

4. Although some consider astrology a science, many others consider it a _____ with no true scientific value.

5. Grow/cultivate and exit/leave are examples of _____.

6. Life/death and succeed/fail are examples of _____.

7. Dale was the _____ leader of the demonstrators, but Bill really made all of the decisions.

*CORRECT OR INCORRECT?*   If the sentence is correct, write a "C" on the line provided. If not, write an "I" for incorrect, then REWRITE the sentence to make it correct. You can change any part of the sentence to make it correct.

1. Joe <u>nominated</u> the conversation and would not let anyone else speak.
   I  dominated

2. You would look in a thesaurus to find a <u>synonym</u> for a word.

   C _____

3. You would look in a thesaurus to find an <u>antonym</u> for a word.

   _____

4. It was important for the president to be <u>anonymous</u>, so he flew into the city on *Air Force One* with a military escort.

   _____

5. When he was applying for a new credit card, Jamie used a <u>pseudonym</u> because he didn't want his parents to find out.

   _____

6. Astronomy is a <u>pseudoscience.</u> Astrology is a true science.

   _____

7. The ad said there would be a <u>nominal</u> fee for shipping, so I was surprised when the fee was more than the cost of the item I ordered.

   C _____

*SHORT ANSWER*   Write your answers on a separate sheet of paper.

1. What characteristics might someone have who would be <u>nominated</u> to be president of an organization at your school? Name the organization and then the qualities.

2. Write a <u>synonym</u> for each of the following words:

   evening/ _night_

   eccentric/ _odd_

   transfer/ _move_

   confer/ _de·_

3. Write an <u>antonym</u> for each of the following words:

   sunlight/ _dark_

   anonymous/ _known_

   anomalous/ _____

   concur/ _disagree_

4. Describe a situation in which a celebrity would want to be <u>anonymous</u>. When might he or she **not** want to be <u>anonymous</u>? Explain your answers.

5. Why would a famous person use a <u>pseudonym</u>? Why would a regular person use one?

6. Draw a Venn diagram to show similarities and differences between <u>pseudoscience</u> and Chemistry.

7. What is a synonym and an antonym for <u>nominal</u>?

# Power Words

1. **empirical**   ĕm-pîr′ĭ-kəl   adjective

   Relying on or derived from observation or experiment

   The researcher used **empirical** evidence that he *got through observing* the children as the basis for his theories on childhood behavior.

*[handwritten annotations: xext &, imply, infer, sender, speak, write, Receiver, Listen, Read]*

2. **imply**  ĭm-plī′  verb

   To express indirectly

   The speaker **implied** that the organization was not managed properly, but he *never directly stated* that opinion.

3. **albatross**  ăl′bə-trôs′  noun

   A constant, worrisome burden; an obstacle to success

   Stephanie never thought that winning the state lottery would be such an **albatross** for her, but her new wealth *caused her to lose friends and her job.*

   **Vocabulary Tip:** An albatross is a Spanish pelican. It is believed that if someone harms this bird, bad luck or misfortune will result.

4. **narcissism**  när′sĭ-sĭz′əm  noun

   Excessive love or admiration of oneself; conceit; a psychological condition characterized by self-preoccupation and lack of empathy

   The boy's **narcissism** was evident when *all he could talk about was himself.*

   **Vocabulary Tip:** The word narcissiam refers to Narcissus, a beautiful youth in Greek mythology who fell in love with his reflection in a pond and was changed into the flower narcissus, which grows near water.

## *Practice Exercises*

1. How could you gather <u>empirical</u> evidence to prove a theory about the importance of eating breakfast before school?

2. Explain the difference between <u>infer</u> and <u>imply</u>.

3. What would be an <u>albatross</u> to your success as a student?

4. If someone were <u>narcissistic</u>, how would he or she act in a job interview?

# Chapter Review

## *Extend Your Learning*

Use one or more of the following exercises to practice the words in this chapter. Remember that it is important to use a variety of strategies in order to maximize your learning.

• Think of a picture in a magazine or a scene in a movie that you can associate with a word from this chapter. For example, visualize a courtroom scene from *Law and Order* in which the crime is solved because of an <u>anonymous</u> tip. Or you could relate one of the shows featuring vampires to the word <u>pseudoscience</u>. Do this for all the words. Write the word and a brief description of the picture or scene.

• Restate out loud the definition for each word in this chapter. Then recite a sentence using the word, trying to make the sentences as personal as possible; that is, for <u>nominate</u> you might think about whom you would like to <u>nominate</u> for president in the next election.

• Construct a tri-fold to learn the words in this chapter. The directions for tri-folds are in Chapter Five.

• Get into a group and create a game of concentration using the words from this chapter. These websites will help you: www.quia.com, www.discoveryschool.com, or similar sites.

*Expanded Word Forms*

nominate      nomination      nominated      infer          inferred
confer         conferring       conference    inferences

1. Jim and Joan were called to school for a _____ about their sixth grade son, Joey. The teacher wanted to _____ with them about his behavior. Unfortunately, while they were _____, Joey hit a baseball through the school window.

2. At the beginning of the senior year, the students were asked to _____ their fellow classmates for several awards. Julie was _____ for the top writing prize. The winning _____ was announced at graduation and, to her pleasure, Julie won the award.

3. One critical reading skill is to be able to _____ what the author is saying when it is not directly stated. Making correct _____ takes time and skill as well as solid background knowledge. The reader must be careful that what he or she has _____ is really what the author means.

*Puzzle Fun*

**Across**

2. insignificant
4. note taker or journalist
6. deduce or derive
8. false science
11. express indirectly
13. alias
15. propose as a candidate
16. a burden or obstacle

**Down**

1. move
3. self-love; conceit
5. deference
7. opposite in meaning
9. derived from observation or experimentation
10. transfer
12. footnote
14. same meaning
17. nameless

# CHAPTER SEVEN
# Remembering New Words

*Handle them carefully, for words have*
*more power than atom bombs.*

Pearl Strachan Hurd, British politician in the 1930s

## CHAPTER OBJECTIVE

**Students will be able to identify and use words with the following common structural elements:**

Roots: gen, duce
Prefixes: pre-, ante-, post-
Suffixes: -cide

## CHAPTER OUTLINE

 **Memory Tip**   Memory Techniques

 **Learning Strategy**   Secondary Rehearsal Strategies (concept maps, outlines, summaries, etc.)

**Part A**
*Words to Learn*

| | |
|---|---|
| genetic | patricide |
| genesis | fratricide |
| genocide | ecocide |
| matricide | |

*Structural Elements*

| | |
|---|---|
| gen | -cide |

**Part B**
*Words to Learn*

| | |
|---|---|
| predict | anteroom |
| prejudice | antecedent |
| induce | postpone |
| postmortem | |

*Structural Elements*

pre-

ante-

post-

duce

*Power Words*

| | |
|---|---|
| deem | vehement |
| contend | misogynist |

### Memory Tip   Memory Techniques: Mnemonics, Association, and Visualization

**Mnemonics** is a memory technique that improves learning at the beginning of the learning process. It is the use of a short word or phrase (usually based on the first letter of each word in a series) that you create to help you remember the series of items by reducing the information to its simplest form. One of the more famous mnemonic devices helps beginning math students remember the order of operations: <u>P</u>lease <u>e</u>xcuse <u>m</u>y <u>d</u>ear <u>A</u>unt <u>S</u>ally, or PEMDAS. This helps students remember to do their calculations in the following order: parentheses, exponents, multiplication, division, addition, subtraction.

When developing a mnemonic you should make a catchword or catchphrase that is personal to you. Be sure to consider whether the information needs to be in a specific order or not. For example, if you were trying to remember the seven steps to improving memory, simply reduce each of the steps to ONE key word. Reduce the key word to a single letter (usually the first letter of the key word). At that point you can develop a catchword—a single word made up of all of the first letters of the key words; or a catch phrase—a sentence that uses all of the initial letters of the key words.

In the following phrases you will find the key words in bold print. Next to each sentence you will find the key word reduced to its simplest form—the first letter of the word. At the end of the list you will see a catchword that was made up from the key words.

### Seven Steps to Improving Memory

1. **Intend** to remember (I)

2. **Organize** the material (O)

3. Test/retest: include **recitation** (R)

4. **Overlearn** the material (O)

5. Use **memory** techniques: mnemonics, association, visualization (M)

6. **Space** your learning over several study sessions (S)

7. Study before **bed** (B)

**Catchword: I. Brooms**

---

(<u>i</u>ntend-<u>b</u>ed-<u>r</u>ecitation-<u>o</u>verlearn-<u>o</u>rganize-<u>m</u>emory-<u>s</u>pace)

---

**Catchphrase:** I owe Ralph or Molly several bucks.

Develop your own catchword or phrase for the seven steps for improving memory. You can use any word in the phrase as your key word. Remember to make it as personal as *you* can to help *you* recall the information.

**Association** and **visualization** are additional tools to help improve memory. The memory technique of association is simply the connection of new concepts to be remembered with those that are already familiar. By association you will create "hooks" that will help you develop expanded learning maps. Visualization is just as it sounds, forming a mental picture of the information.

### Learning Strategy   Secondary Rehearsal Strategies (SRS)

SRS are used to consolidate textbook and lecture information. These strategies help students achieve over learning. Examples of commonly used SRSs are timelines, outlines, webs/maps, study guides, and summaries. These strategies will assist you in condensing textbook and lecture information into as few as three to six study pages.

In earlier chapters you reviewed strategies that helped you to begin the learning/memory process. These strategies are called Primary Rehearsal Strategies (PRS). Once the material is introduced and rehearsed, it is necessary to complete the learning/memory process by locking the information into your long-term memory. By using one or more of the Secondary Rehearsal Strategies (SRS), you can achieve this goal.

**Secondary Rehearsal Strategies**

| Strategy | Description | Suggested Disciplines |
|---|---|---|
| *Timeline* | After surveying the chapter, determine where the chapter information begins and ends. Develop a timeline that indicates the progression of the information. | Social Sciences Literature |
| *Outline* | Follow the chapter headings and subheadings, and record the information in a traditional outline format. | Humanities Social Sciences Natural Sciences |
| *Map/Web* | Prepare a visual representation of the same information that is on an outline. This provides the learner with a picture of the information. | Humanities Social Sciences Natural Sciences |
| *Study Guides* | Group the important information according to heading such as people, places, dates, topics provided by the instructor, and learning objectives in the textbook chapter. | Any academic course |
| *Summaries* | Find the main topic in the chapter. For each section of text, write a brief account of the information. Opinions are omitted. | Any academic course |

# Part A

 ***WORDS TO LEARN—SEE AND SAY*** Use the pronunciation guide on the first page of this book to help you SAY each word.

1. genetic        jə-nĕt'ĭk
2. genesis        jĕn'ĭ-sĭs
3. genocide        jĕn'ə-sīd'
4. matricide        măt'rĭ-sīd'
5. patricide        păt'rĭ-sīd'
6. fratricide        frăt'rĭ-sīd'
7. ecocide        ē'kō-sīd'

*duct*

 ***STRUCTURAL ELEMENTS*** Look at the structural elements of each word. Use these elements to unlock the word's meaning.

| | |
|---|---|
| gen | birth, beginning; group or kind |
| -cide | to kill, murder |

***CONTEXT CLUES*** Read the sentences. Use the words around the unfamiliar word to determine the word's meaning. Words in bold are the vocabulary words; words in italic are the context clues.

1. Do you think it will ever be possible to alter *basic human* **genetic** material in order to produce the perfect human being?

2. While discussing the song's **genesis** in her autobiography, she stated that she *began to write it* one night in a Dublin bar.

3. When the conquering army found *mass graves*, the country's top military officers were arrested for **genocide.**

4. Mrs. Brown was the oldest member of the family. When she was *murdered by her daughter*, the act of **matricide** was devastating to everyone.

5. Jeff was suspected of **patricide** because he was the last person with his *father before his murder*.

6. There was a trial in my county last year in which one brother was convicted of **fratricide** for *killing his twin*.

7. Jenna was very conscious of the environment, so the **ecocide** that *destroyed the forest* near her home as a result of the strip mining was very upsetting.

 *DICTIONARY*   Read the following definitions.

1. **genetic**   adjective/noun

   **Etymology:** gen (birth, kind, beginning, or race) ic (relates to or pertains to)

   (adjective) Of, relating to, or influenced by the origin or development of something

   The child's **genetic** *make-up* determined her *height* and *hair color*.

   (noun) biology dealing with heredity and variation; that which one inherits

   The cancer doctor was interested in whether the disease was more *prevalent in family groups*, so he added a specialist to his practice to study the **genetics** of the disease.

2. **genesis**   noun

   **Etymology:** gen (birth, race, or beginning)

   The coming into being of something; the origin

   The **genesis** of my career was when I took my neighbor's dog to the veterinarian; *I knew then* that I wanted to be a vet.

   **Synonyms:** birth, beginning

   **Antonym:** end

3. **genocide**   noun

   **Etymology:** gen (race, kind, beginning, birth) cide (kill)

   The killing of a group, race, or kind

   One of the most notorious acts of **genocide** was the *mass killings* in Germany during WWII.

   **Synonym:** mass murder

4. **matricide**   noun

   **Etmology:** matre (mother) cide (kill)

   The act of killing one's mother

   When *Mrs. Jones was found dead* in her basement, the first *suspect* was her estranged *daughter* who had recently visited her. She was suspected of committing **matricide**.

5. **patricide**   noun

   **Etymology:** patre (father) cide (kill)

   The act of killing one's father

   No one suspected Jeff of **patricide** when his *father was found dead* since it seemed like the two were best friends.

6. **fratricide**   noun

   **Etymology:** frater (brother, sibling) cide (kill)

   The crime of killing one's brother or sister

   The prisoner was sentenced to life without parole for his terrible act of **fratricide**—*he killed his three younger siblings*.

7. **ecocide**   noun

**Etymology:** eco (habitat or environment) cide (kill)

Destruction of the natural environment, as by pollutants or an act of war

Environmentalists are always warning countries about possible **ecocide** *as a long-term result of chemical warfare.*

## *Practice Exercises*

### *MULTIPLE CHOICE*

1. The crime of <u>matricide</u> involves which of the following?
   a. poisoning a mother
   b. taking a mother to dinner for her birthday
   c. attending a dance recital with the star dancer's mother
   d. taking food to a mother when she is ill

2. The <u>genesis</u> of an idea happens
   a. at the middle of the process
   b. at the end
   c. at the beginning of the process
   d. spaced equally throughout the process

3. Which of the following characteristics are <u>genetic</u>?
   a. the number of traffic tickets you received
   b. hair and eye color
   c. your grade in basic chemistry
   d. your hairstyle

4. What would happen if someone committed <u>patricide</u>?
   a. He or she would get a promotion in the family owned company.
   b. His or her mother would be a widow
   c. He or she would buy a new car.
   d. He or she would take his or her father to the movies.

5. If you systematically destroyed a group of people from the same culture, you committed
   a. infanticide
   b. fratricide
   c. genocide
   d. pesticide

6. If someone kills his brother and sister, he commits
   a. infanticide
   b. fratricide
   c. genocide
   d. pesticide

7. Which of the following would be eliminated by an act of <u>ecocide</u>?
   a. transfat in fast-food french fries
   b. your mother and father
   c. a 100-year-old forest
   d. an entire ethnic group

*FILL IN THE BLANK*   Select the BEST word for each sentence. Use each word only once.

genetics ②   genesis ③ ✓   genocide ⑤ ✓   matricide ①
4 patricide ①   fratricide ④ ✓   ecocide ⑥ ✓

1. The acts of _____ and _____ involve killing a parent.

2. The doctors studied the _____ of the disability in order to be able to predict who might be prone to developing it as they got older.

3. The _____ of the idea for the new product came from a meeting that was held long before anyone knew there would be such a demand for the item.

4. In a newspaper story last week, I read about a young man who was convicted of _____ after murdering his sister.

5. If a dictator eliminated all of the members of the opposing political party, he would be guilty of _____.

6. Many people see global warming as an example of _____.

*CORRECT OR INCORRECT?*   If the sentence is correct, write a "C" on the line provided. If not, write an "I" for incorrect, then REWRITE the sentence to make it correct. You can change any part of the sentence to make it correct.

1. Bill was convicted of <u>matricide</u> after killing his father and <u>patricide</u> for the murder of his mother.
   I _____ mother _____ father _____

2. The doctor diagnosed the <u>genetic</u> illness as being caused by an unhealthy lifestyle.
   I _____

3. At its <u>genesis</u>, the plan seemed simple and effective; it was only after it was put into effect that the complexities became apparent.
   C _____

4. Tim's younger brother annoyed him so much that he fantasized about <u>fratricide</u>.
   C _____

5. I was so frustrated by the traffic jam when I was headed to the football game that I dreamed of committing <u>ecocide</u> and eliminating all of the other drivers on the road.
   I _____ genocide _____

6. I enjoy reading horror novels, but not ones where vampires commit <u>genocide</u> when they repeatedly stalk single young women at night.
   I _____

*SHORT ANSWER*   Write your answers on a separate sheet of paper.

1. In Chapter Three you learned that *arch* means ruler. Put the word parts *matri* and *patri* each together with *arch* to form a word that means the person who is the head of a family. Who would this person be in your family?

2. What <u>genetic</u> characteristics did you get from your parents? List at least three.

3. What are two other words or phrases that mean the same as <u>genesis</u>?

4. How are the words <u>ecocide</u> and <u>genocide</u> both similar and different?

5. Create a word map using the words from this section with the suffix *-cide*. Put *-cide* in the middle and the words and definitions as spokes radiating out from the center. Add <u>homicide</u> and <u>suicide</u> or any other word that you know to your word map.

6. Take the word part *-cide* and add it to other words to make nonsense words about what you would like to eliminate. For example, someone who is tired of technology might form the word *technocide*.

## Part B

 ***WORDS TO LEARN—SEE AND SAY***   Use the pronunciation guide on the first page of this book to help you SAY each word.

1. predict          prĭ-dĭkt′
2. prejudice        prĕj′ə-dĭs
3. induce           ĭn-dōōs′
4. anteroom         ăn′tē-rōōm′
5. antecedent       ăn′tĭ-sēd′nt
6. postmortem       pōst-môr′təm
7. postpone         pōs(t)-′pōn

*(handwritten) (ir)responsible   Prefix   Suffix*

***STRUCTURAL ELEMENTS***   Look at the structural elements of each word. Use these elements to unlock the word's meaning.

| | |
|---|---|
| pre- | before |
| ante- | before |
| post- | after |
| duce | to lead |

***CONTEXT CLUES***   Read the sentences. Use the words around the unfamiliar word to determine the word's meaning. Words in bold are the vocabulary words; words in italic are the context clues.

1. The fortune-teller **predicted** the flood *weeks before* it actually happened.
2. Many women still encounter extreme **prejudice** in the workplace, which *prevents them from achieving executive positions.*
3. The impressive television advertisements **induced** me *to buy a new car.*
4. The pediatrician's **anteroom** was where the parents and children waited *before going into the doctor's actual office.*
5. The **antecedent** to the success of the play was a great dress rehearsal *the night before it opened.*
6. The results of the **postmortem** tests showed that the young man had *died* of cyanide poisoning.
7. Because of the predicted storm, the class picnic was **postponed** *until later in the week.*

***DICTIONARY***   Read the following definitions.

1. **predict**   verb

   **Etymology:** pre (before) dict (speak or say)

   To foretell something; prophesy

   *Before* I even started to learn to drive, my mother **predicted** that I would fail my driving test the first time, and she was right.

   **Synonyms:** forecast, conclude

2. **prejudice**   noun/verb

   **Etymology:** pre (before) jud (judge) ice (make or cause to be) (noun) An unfair and unreasonable opinion or feeling when formed without enough thought or knowledge

Dr. Jones held a strong **prejudice** *against females* in his chemistry class and did not give them as much help during labs as he did the males. *I prjudge before I see him*

(verb) To influence unfairly so that an unreasonable opinion is formed

Dr. Jones also **prejudiced** his graduate assistants *against female chemistry majors.*

**Synonym:** bias, intolerance

3. **induce**   verb

**Etymology:** in (into) duce (lead)

To lead or move, as to a course of action, by influence or persuasion

The president's State of the Union address **induced**, or *encouraged*, me to become part of his reelection team for his second term.

**Synomyn:** persuade

**Vocabulary Tip:** *Induce* is a great word to use in general to describe persuading or convincing someone to act. For example: "See if you can induce Sally to participate in the program with you."

4. **anteroom**   noun

**Etymology:** ante (before) room (room)

An outer room that opens into another room, often used as a waiting room

There were so many people waiting to register for the 5K race that some had to wait *outside the main office,* in the **anteroom,** until there was more space.

5. **antecedent**   noun

**Etymology:** ante (before) ced (to send) ent (relates to)

A preceding occurrence, cause, or event; going before; preceding

Joan noticed that the **antecedent** to all of the exams where she earned an A was attending the *pre-exam* review sessions offered by the professors.

6. **postmortem**   adjective/noun

**Etymology:** post (after) mort (death) em (relates to)

(adjective) Occurring or done after death

*After the failed* sales campaign, the advertising team held a **postmortem** meeting to determine what had gone wrong.

(noun) a discussion or analysis of an event after it is over

A **postmortem** was conducted *after the patient's death* to determine the cause.

7. **postpone**   verb

**Etymology:** post (after) pon (put or place)

To delay until a future time

Why would you want to **postpone** your meeting *until next week* when you have everything ready and everyone is waiting for you now?

**Synonym:** delay

**Antonyms:** speed up, accelerate

*Practice Exercises*

*MULTIPLE CHOICE*

1. A student treated with <u>prejudice</u> might
   a. be given a lower grade than she earned
   b. be treated the same as everyone else
   c. be elected homecoming king or queen
   d. get to go home on the weekend to visit his friends

2. What is something you might <u>predict</u>?
   a. how you inherited your hair color
   b. what type of job you will get after graduation
   c. why your professor canceled class
   d. how many hours you spent studying for finals last semester

3. Where would you find an <u>anteroom</u>?
   a. in a doctor's office
   b. at your local park
   c. at McDonald's
   d. in your bedroom at home

4. Which of the following would be an <u>antecedent</u> to a conference?
   a. a wrap-up session on the last day
   b. a coffee break scheduled between speakers
   c. a survey sent to participants after they returned home
   d. a planning meeting to schedule the speakers

5. When you <u>induce</u> someone to do something against his or her will, you are
   a. following along with what he or she originally wanted to do
   b. trying to persuade someone to do something he or she doesn't want to do
   c. trying to win an argument
   d. changing your mind and doing what someone else wants

6. When would a <u>postmortem</u> meeting be scheduled?
   a. before the event happened
   b. after the project failed and was canceled
   c. during the initial planning stage
   d. to troubleshoot during the event

7. Why would you <u>postpone</u> a wedding?
   a. because the bride and groom were dressed and the church was full of wedding guests
   b. because the bride and groom had already booked a cruise for their honeymoon
   c. because the bride and groom were not sure they wanted to get married
   d. because the invitations had been received by the guests six weeks in advance of the date

*FILL IN THE BLANK*   Select the BEST word for each sentence. Use each word only once.

predict          induce          anteroom          antecedent
prejudice        postpone        postmortem

1. There are laws in our country that prohibit treating people with _____ and denying them their basic rights.

2. Before meeting with the Board of Directors, the candidates for the CEO position waited in the _____ until the previous interview was over.

3. The group study session was a(n) _____ to the midterm exam.

4. Because of the mysterious circumstances surrounding the patient's death, all the people involved in the patient's care were required to attend a _____ meeting.

5. The fortune-teller told the girl that she could _____ the future and tell her whom she would marry.

6. None of the students were prepared for the exam; therefore, the professor decided to _____ it until the next class.

7. Jill tried to _____ Mike to skip class and go shopping, but he knew there would be a review for the midterm and did not want to miss it.

*CORRECT OR INCORRECT?*   If the sentence is correct, write a "C" on the line provided. If not, write an "I" for incorrect, then REWRITE the sentence to make it correct. You can change any part of the sentence to make it correct.

1. The doctor was able to accurately <u>predict</u> how long the patient had not been feeling well.

   _I_____

2. The small <u>anteroom</u> that you entered prior to entering the gym helped keep the cold air out when the outside door was opened.

   _C_____

3. The <u>antecedent</u> following the traffic accident had the purpose of making the intersection safer.

   _I_____

4. Joe was <u>induced</u> by the police for the robbery that happened two blocks from his house.

   _I_____

5. The entire freshman class felt that there was <u>prejudice</u> against them when they were welcomed onto the campus the first day and made to feel at home.

   _I_____

6. Before every transplant surgery, the lead surgeon gathered the team of doctors and nurses for a <u>postmortem</u> clinic.

   _I_____

7. Jill was excited to celebrate her eighth birthday and couldn't wait to <u>postpone</u> her party until the next week.

   _I_____

*SHORT ANSWER*   Write your answers on a separate sheet of paper.

1. Many people make <u>predictions</u>. What would be necessary for a prediction to be considered reliable?

2. Name three locations that might have an <u>anteroom</u>.

3. What would you consider a memorable <u>antecedent</u> to celebrate someone starting his or her college education?

4. Describe an example of <u>prejudice</u> in our country.

5. If you held a <u>postmortem</u> session after you failed a course, what would you consider?

6. Describe a situation when you might try to <u>induce</u> someone to do what you want.

7. Name three reasons someone might <u>postpone</u> going to college after he or she graduated from high school.

# Power Words

1. **deem**   dēm   verb

   Believe or consider to be true

   If a teacher **deems** a child ready for first grade, *then she will promote him.*

   **Synonym:** presume

   **Antonym:** doubt

   **Vocabulary Tip:** *Deem* is derived from the Old English *deman*, which means "to pass judgment." If you deem something, it means you have judged it. The literal meaning for *deem* is "to hold to be true." (www.vocabulary-vocabulary.com)

2. **contend**   kən-těnd´   verb   *clean something / compete w/t someone*

   Assert to be true; strive against rivals or difficulties

   Once Muhammad Ali decided to **contend** for the heavyweight title, he practiced several times each day to ensure that he would be *ready for the contest.*

   **Synonym:** maintain, battle

   **Vocabulary Tip:** *Contend* is derived from the Latin word *contendere*, "to stretch out or strive after." Think of what a fighter or boxer does as he is a contender for the win. He stretches or strives after the win.

3. **vehement**   vē´ə-mənt   adjective   *hard working, Put her hole energy to something*

   Characterized by forcefulness of expression; marked by or full of vigor and energy

   Joan's **vehement** desire to succeed is obvious by the way she *studiously prepares* for exams.

   **Synonyms:** fervent, passionate

   **Vocabulary Tip:** *Vehement* is from Latin and was origially applied to intense natural phenomena: pain, heat, wind, etc. It is now more commonly used for intense emotions or beliefs. With the adverb form, the most common usage is used when people are vehemently opposed to something. (www.vocabulary-vocabulary.com)

4. **misogynist**   mĭ-sŏj´ə-nĭst   noun

   One who hates women; one who displays prejudice against women

   The part the actor portrayed in the play was of a **misogynist**, but in real life he was very much *the opposite, he loved women.*

## Practice Exercise

1. Write a paragraph or short story using the preceding four words. Include context clues to help the reader understand the meaning of the words.

# Chapter Review

## Extend Your Learning

Use one or more of the following exercises to practice the words in this chapter. Remember that it is important to use a variety of strategies in order to maximize your learning.

- Look for pictures in magazines that you could use to illustrate some of the words in this chapter. In some cases you will need to find pictures that will enable you to create a story to illustrate the word. For example, if you find a picture of someone looking thoughtful, you can create a story about the person predicting what will happen in an imaginary situation.

- Read the words, definitions, and sample sentences into a voice recorder. Listen to the recording as you drive or are doing other tasks where you can listen.
- Make a tri-fold for the words in Parts A and B and the Power Words.
- Write the words on index cards, one word per card. Mix them up, then reorder them into groups according to word parts. Next, develop sentences using as many words as you can in one sentence. As you do this, put those word cards together in one pile.

## *Expanded Word Forms*

Select the appropriate word form for each of the sentences.

predict        prediction        predicting        postpone        postponing        postponed

1. Because I am so busy, I was thinking about _____ my dentist appointment, but I realized that if I _____ the appointment I would have trouble scheduling another one. Why would I _____ the appointment and then reschedule another one in a day or two?

2. The office of admissions can closely _____ how many students will enroll each semester because of the software that it has incorporated that is in line with the county statistical board information. This _____ will help the school in preparing schedules and budgets that will assist the school's financial security. _____ how many classes will be needed greatly improves the class planning and scheduling.

*Puzzle Fun*

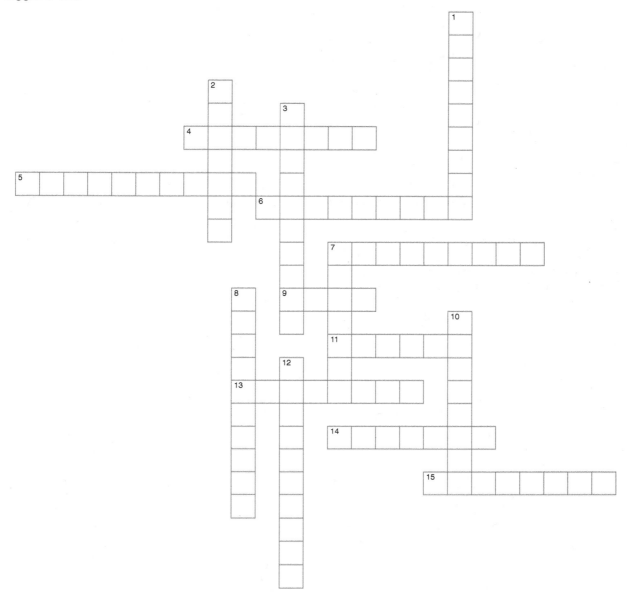

**Across**

4. might be like a foyer or a waiting or receiving area
5. can occur only after someone's demise or death
6. intolerance of others
7. an unspeakable act against one's father is this
9. if you totally believe something to be true
11. persuade or convince someone to act
13. if you are planning on starting a family you might be very interested in this
14. the beginning or birth of something would be known as this
15. fervent or very passionate in one's speech or feelings as they are displayed

**Down**

1. an unspeakable act against one's mother is this
2. if you assert that something is true
3. you may not like your brother or sister but you should never consider this
7. a "prophet" or a "prophecy" may do this
8. you certainly wouldn't be looking for a wife or girlfriend if you happen to be this
10. what happened in Nazi Germany
12. something coming before or sent before

# CHAPTER EIGHT

# No Unlearning Allowed!
# Use It or Lose It!

*Not to unlearn what you have learned.*

Diogenes Laertius (third century A.D.), upon being
asked what learning was the most necessary

## CHAPTER OBJECTIVE

**Students will be able to identify and use words with the following common structural elements:**

Roots: ped, pod, graph
Prefixes: phile-, philo-, trans-, auto-
Suffixes: -agogue

## CHAPTER OUTLINE

 **Memory Tip**   Study Before Bed

 **Learning Strategy**   Frequency of Forgetting

**Part A**
*Words to Learn*

| | |
|---|---|
| pediatric | podium |
| pedophile | pedagogy |
| podiatrist | bibliophile |
| pedestal | technophile |

*Structural Elements*

| | |
|---|---|
| ped | pod |
| -agogue | |
| phile-, philo- | |

**Part B**
*Words to Learn*

| | |
|---|---|
| transmit | transformation |
| transient | autonomy |
| demography | autograph |
| graphology | autobiography |

*Structural Elements*

trans-
auto-
graph

*Power Words*

| | |
|---|---|
| annotate | extrovert |
| introvert | paraphrase |

## 💡 *Memory Tip*   Study Before Bed

Remembering can be enhanced by eliminating interference: therefore, you should try to eliminate distractions while studying. One strategy is to study before bed and then go directly to sleep—do not talk to family or friends and do not watch TV—in order to improve your retention of the material. Upon awakening, review the material one more time.

## 🔍 *Learning Strategy*   Frequency of Forgetting

Short review sessions are an effective way to enhance remembering. In previous chapters you were introduced to Primary Rehearsal Strategies (PRS) that include tri-folds and concept cards. Use these strategies when doing short review sessions.

Along with remembering, we should also be aware of the frequency of forgetting. The following illustration indicates the amount of forgetting that occurs and the rate at which it occurs. Forgetting typically occurs rapidly. Within the first 24 hours of being introduced to material, you will forget about 25% of what you learned. Within 48 hours, you can forget 75%. After reviewing the following illustration, you will see that just 10 minutes of review a day will greatly increase the amount of material that is retained.

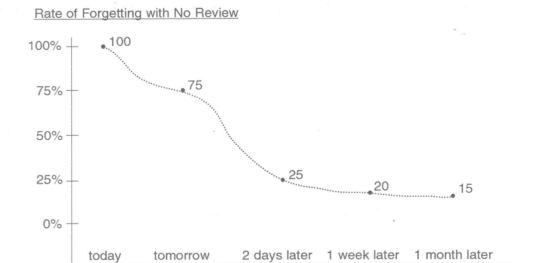

Rate of Forgetting with No Review

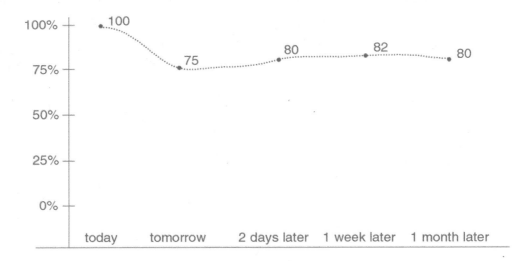

Rate of Forgetting when 10 Minutes of Review Per Day Is Added

# Part A

 *WORDS TO LEARN—SEE AND SAY*    Use the pronunciation guide on the first page of this book to help you SAY each word.

1. pediatric          pĕ′dē-ăt′rĭk (adjective),    pediatrician   pĕ′dē-ă-trĭsh′ən (noun)

2. pedophile         pĕd′ə-fīl′

3. podiatrist        pə-dī′ə-trĭst

4. pedestal          pĕd′ĭ-stəl

5. podium            pō′də-əm

6. pedagogy          pĕd′ə-gō′jē

7. bibliophile       bĭb′lē- ə-fīl′

8. technophile       tĕk′nə-fīl′

 *STRUCTURAL ELEMENTS*    Look at the structural elements of each word. Use these elements to unlock the word's meaning.

| | |
|---|---|
| ped | child, foot |
| pod | foot |
| -agogue *person* | leader of |
| phile-, philo- | love of |

 *CONTEXT CLUES*    Read the sentences. Use the words around the unfamiliar word to determine the word's meaning. Words in bold are the vocabulary words; words in italic are the context clues.

1. The United Way funded the new **pediatric** clinic for the care and well-being of the *young children* of Nigeria.

2. The most egregious, or terrible, crime of all is the crime that a **pedophile** *commits on a young child.*

3. The **podiatrist** warned the young model about the harmful effects that high-heeled shoes can have on her *feet.*

4. The Tiffany lamp was embellished, or adorned, with a gold-leaf **pedestal**. The *base* was as beautiful as the Tiffany lampshade.

5. The band conductor was told not to overload the **podium** with his books and music because the *structure* was not sturdy enough.

6. **Pedagogy**, *the art of teaching*, can only be mastered through years of study and a genuine desire to help children.

7. Gina's *love of books* clearly meant she was a **bibliophile**.

8. Our office manager is a **technophile**; she *has every new electronic device* that comes out.

*DICTIONARY*    Read the following definitions.

1. pediatric    adjective

**Etymology:** ped (child) ic (relates or pertains to)

Related to the medical care and treatment of children

Mrs. Smith, a **pediatric** nurse at Memorial General Hospital, received an award for the most outstanding *care of the infants* there in 1999.

**Antonym:** geriatric

**pediatrician**   noun

A doctor who cares for children

Dr. Jones is the **pediatrician** who cared for all five of my *children* from the time they were born until they went to high school.

2. **pedophile**   noun

**Etymology:** ped (child) phile (love of)

An adult who is sexually attracted to children; a child molester

It is very unnerving to read about the **pedophile** who is lurking around our elementary schools; most parents want to keep their children at home where they are *safe from such vicious predators.*

**Synonym:** child molester

3. **podiatrist**   noun   *a person who treat the person foot*

**Etymology:** pod (foot) iatrist (someone who heals)

One who cares for disorders or treatment of the feet

Dr. Smith is an excellent **podiatrist**. When I *broke my foot* he was gentle yet thorough in his care.

**Vocabulary Tip:** The structural element –*ist* means "someone who or something that." The suffix -*iatrist* is more specific and means "a person who heals."

4. **pedestal**   noun   *object*

**Etymology:** ped (foot) al (relates to or pertains to)

An architectural support or base for a column or statue

After I let my dog into the house, she ran around so quickly that she knocked over the **pedestal** that *held my valuable lamp* and broke both the lamp and the pedestal.

**Synonyms:** base, foundation, foot

**Vocabulary Tip:** Pedestal refers to feet because the bottom of something is generally called the foot or base.

5. **podium**   noun   *Person stand on it, or behind it*

**Etymology:** pod (foot) ium (relates to or house of)

An elevated platform for an orchestra conductor or public speaker; a stand for holding notes or music

The students knew the lecture would begin as soon as the professor *stepped up to the* **podium** and arranged his notes in front of him.

**Synonyms:** dais, lectern

6. **pedagogy**   noun

**Etymology:** ped (child) agague (leader of)

The art or profession of teaching children

**Pedagogy** is a skill that is best taught as a hands-on lesson. It isn't until you are in front of a classroom that you have the complete understanding of the *art of teaching.*

**Synonym:** instruction

7. **bibliophile**   noun

**Etymology:** biblio (books) phile (love of)

A lover or collector of books

*After spending every evening for the past month in the new bookstore, Gina was obviously seen as a true* **bibliophile**.

8. **technophile** noun

**Etymology:** tech (technology) phile (love of)

One who has a love of or enthusiasm for technology, especially computers and high technology

*Steve Jobs and Bill Gates are perfect examples of* **technophiles**.

## *Practice Exercises*

### *MULTIPLE CHOICE*

1. Of the following, which is the most likely place you would find a <u>pediatric</u> nurse?
   a. at a professional sports team's training camp
   b. at an elementary school
   c. at a rock concert
   d. at a community college

2. A <u>pedophile</u> tries to harm
   a. young children
   b. people's feet
   c. the art displayed on top of it
   d. fingernails

3. Why would you go to a <u>podiatrist</u>?
   a. to have your fingernails painted
   b. to arrest him for child pornography
   c. to have an ingrown toenail treated
   d. to learn how to teach

4. Why would you need a <u>pedestal</u>?
   a. to get an ingrown toenail treated
   b. to support and display an expensive vase
   c. to hold your notes for a speech you are giving
   d. to care for a sick child

5. Why would you need a <u>podium</u>?
   a. to get an ingrown toenail treated
   b. to support and display an expensive vase
   c. to hold your notes for a speech you are giving
   d. to care for a sick child

6. Which of the following is an example of <u>pedagogy</u>?
   a. waiting until you have the entire class's attention before starting to speak
   b. knowing the fastest route to drive to school
   c. lending money to students who lost their lunch pass
   d. always having enough pens and pencils

7. Where would you find a <u>bibliophile</u>?
   a. Willi's Ski Shop
   b. the Apple Store looking at the latest computer
   c. Barnes & Noble book store
   d. Baskin-Robbins ice cream shop

8. Where would you find a <u>technophile</u>?
   a. Willi's Ski Shop
   b. the Apple Store looking at the latest computer
   c. Barnes & Noble book store
   d. Baskin-Robbins ice cream shop

*FILL IN THE BLANK*   Select the BEST word for each sentence. Use each word only once.

pediatric ⑤   pedophile ⑥   podiatrist ①   pedestal ③
podium ⑦   pedagogy ④   bibliophile ②   technophile ⑧

1. The _____ told Sue she would need an operation to fix her broken foot before she could run in another marathon.

2. Dale had to buy a new bookcase because he is a _____ and has more books than room to store them.

3. The entire school was so proud of the trophy won by the girls' basketball team that it purchased a special _____ to display it on.

4. The inept student teacher was not able to graduate because of her poor evaluations in _____.

5. Because he was only three, Sam stayed on the _____ wing when he had his tonsils removed.

6. After preying on innocent children and teenagers, the _____ was sent to jail for the remainder of his life.

7. The keynote speaker fell and was seriously injured when the _____ he was leaning on while speaking broke apart.

8. My friends tease me and call me a _____ just because I always run out and buy the latest electronic tablet the day it is released.

*CORRECT OR INCORRECT?*   If the sentence is correct, write a "C" on the line provided. If not, write an "I" for incorrect, then REWRITE the sentence to make it correct. You can change any part of the sentence to make it correct.

1. The <u>pedophile</u> was convicted and sentenced to 25 years for embezzlement.
   I _____

2. Sally went to the <u>podiatrist</u> for a manicure.
   I _____

3. At the art museum, most of the smaller pieces of sculpture are displayed on <u>podiums</u>.
   I _____

4. The main speaker asked for a <u>pedestal</u> so that she would have someplace to put the notes for her speech.
   I _____

5. Besides getting one or more degrees in teaching, the first grade teacher has been to many conferences to improve his <u>pedagogy</u>.
   C _____

6. My family says I am a <u>technophile</u> because I am always updating my computer and cell phone.
   C _____

7. I am proud to be called a <u>bibliophile</u> because I can never have enough shoes.
   I _____

8. Because the family had always been interested in geriatric diseases of the elderly, they donated money to build a new <u>pediatric</u> wing for the hospital.
   I _____

*SHORT ANSWER*   Write your answers on a separate sheet of paper.

1. Why would a <u>pediatric</u> nurse need more specialized training?

2. What crimes could a <u>pedophile</u> commit using the Internet? How might the police find him or her?

3. Name two reasons why you might go to a <u>podiatrist</u>.

4. There is a saying that a girl wants to date a boy who will "put her on a <u>pedestal</u>." What does this mean? What does the girl want?

5. Who would use a <u>podium</u>? Why?

6. If you are studying to be a teacher, what is one aspect of <u>pedagogy</u> you might learn?

7. Use the suffix *-phile* and create new words to identify what you love to do. For example, you might say that you are a footballphile if you love football.

# Part B

 *WORDS TO LEARN—SEE AND SAY* Use the pronunciation guide on the first page of this book to help you SAY each word.

1. transmit        trăns-mĭt

2. transient        trăn′zē-ənt

3. demography        dĭ-mŏg′rə-fē

4. graphology        gră-fŏl′ə-jē

5. transformation        trăns′fər-mā′shən

6. autonomy        ô-tŏn′ə-mē

7. autograph        ô-tŏg′rə-fē

8. autobiography        ô′tō-bī-ŏg′rə-fē

*STRUCTURAL ELEMENTS* Look at the structural elements of each word. Use these elements to unlock the word's meaning.

| trans- | across |
| auto- | self |
| graph | written |

 *CONTEXT CLUES* Read the sentences. Use the words around the unfamiliar word to determine the word's meaning. Words in bold are the vocabulary words; words in italic are the context clues.

1. Mike called his parents from college for money. His parents immediately **transmitted** the money electronically *into his bank account*.

2. The **transient** beauty that the young debutant *once had was obviously waning as the* years passed.

3. When Sally was looking for a college she looked at the **demography** of each one. *For example, she wanted to know how large the campus was, how many students, how many majors, etc.*

4. Megan is a **graphology** expert and is hired to go to parties to *analyze the guests' handwriting* for entertainment.

5. The butterfly's **transformation** *from a caterpillar to a butterfly* happened almost overnight.

6. Each sorority had **autonomy**; each one *made decisions independently* of the other groups.

7. The football shirt **autographed** *by Ben Roethlisberger* is my most prized possession.

8. I prefer to read the **autobiographies** written by famous leaders so that I am *reading exactly their thoughts* and not someone else's.

*DICTIONARY*    Read the following definitions.

1. **transmit**   verb

   **Etymology:** trans (across) mit (send)

   To send from one person, thing, or place to another

   The photographer **transmitted** the wedding pictures *via the Internet* the day after the wedding.

   **Synonyms:** send, convey

2. **transient**   adjective/noun

   **Etymology:** trans (across) ent (relates to or pertains to)

   (adjective) Remaining in place only a brief time

   **Transient** workers usually *move frequently* as one job ends and another begins.

   (noun) One who moves from place to place; one who does not stay in any one place for a long period of time

   The **transient** was unable to establish a permanent address as he *was always moving* from place to place.

   **Synonyms:** fleeting, not permanent, passing

3. **demography**   noun

   **Etymology:** demo (people) graphy (something written)

   The study of the characteristics of human populations, such as size, growth, density, distribution, and vital statistics.

   The **demography** of the town changed over the years as the *population grew older* and the *young people left to find jobs.*

4. **graphology**   noun

   **Etymology:** graph (written) ology (science or study of)

   The study of handwriting, especially when employed as a means of analyzing character

   **Graphology** analyzes the thickness of *letters* and the *slant* the writer uses when *writing* to *determine personality* or other character traits.

5. **transformation**   noun

   **Etymology:** trans (across) form (form) tion (act, state or condition of)

   A marked change, as in appearance or character, usually for the better

   President Nixon's *visit led to* a **transformation** of American attitudes toward China.

6. **autonomy**   noun   *take care about yourselve*

   **Etymology:** auto (self) nomos (custom or law)

   A self-governing state, community, group, or individual

   Usually by the age of 21 many young people experience a need for **autonomy**, to be able to make *decisions for themselves* and define the rules instead of being dependent on their parents.

7. **autograph**   noun

   **Etymology:** auto (self) graph (written)

   The writing of something in one's own handwriting, usually a greeting and/or name

   Many baseball card collectors know which **autographs** are valuable and which *signatures* are not.

*big*

8. **autobiography**    noun

**Etymology:** auto (self) bio (life or living) graphy (something written)

The story of a person's life written by that person

If you plan to *write your* **autobiography** after you finish college, it would be helpful to make detailed notes while you go through school.

**Synonym:** memoir

## Practice Exercises

### MULTIPLE CHOICE

1. Which of the following is <u>transient</u>?
   a. a house
   b. a hobo
   c. a dentist
   d. an accountant

2. Which of the following is a way diseases are <u>transmitted</u>?
   a. by fast food
   b. by people washing their hands frequently
   c. by people not washing their hands and touching infected objects
   d. by people not exercising and not eating properly.

3. Which of the following would be included in a <u>demography</u> of an area?
   a. the number of state parks in the area
   b. how long it takes to drive to the nearest large city
   c. how many people live there
   d. the number of state highways in the area

4. What would someone do if he or she were a student of <u>graphology</u>?
   a. ask you to write a sample sentence
   b. ask you to speak into a recording device
   c. ask you to walk so he or she could examine your stride
   d. ask you to repeat back a series of numbers

5. Which of the following might precede someone's sudden <u>transformation</u>?
   a. going to the grocery store
   b. switching from regular to decaf coffee
   c. starting to read the newspaper daily
   d. a trip to the spa and hair salon

6. What decision would you make if you had personal <u>autonomy</u>?
   a. how your taxes are spent
   b. whether to go to college or not
   c. how much you would pay in taxes
   d. which restaurant your friend prefers to celebrate her birthday

7. Where is a common location for people to get <u>autographs</u>?
   a. at the mall
   b. at the grocery store
   c. as players leave the locker room after a game
   d. when you are on vacation and never see anyone you know

8. Which of the following might be a first sentence in an <u>autobiography</u>?
   a. Once long ago there was a fairy princess . . .
   b. The easiest way to change a tire is to . . .
   c. I have always been interested in George Washington and want to tell you about his life.
   (d.) I have had many interesting events in my life that are important to the person I have become.

*FILL IN THE BLANK*   Select the BEST word for each sentence. Use each word only once.

transmit ④        demography ②     graphology ⑤      autonomy ⑧
transient ①       transformation ⑦  autobiography ⑥   autograph ③

1. The _____ professor did not have a permanent office because he was only at the college for one semester.

2. Before deciding where to build their new restaurant, the owners researched the _____ of the area to be sure there would be enough people to support another restaurant.

3. I treasure my new book because I have the author's _____ written next to his printed name on the cover page.

4. The bank asked me to _____ my account information to it by fax so it can help me find the mistake in my balance.

5. Through the study of _____, Amy was able to describe the criminal's personality by examining the handwritten ransom note.

6. When the previous president's book was published about his life, the bookstore filled the front window with a huge display of the _____.

7. The stray puppy's _____ was dramatic after being fed and shampooed at the kennel.

8. Because the members of the community organization had _____ they could decide when and how often to hold meetings without asking for permission from the township.

*CORRECT OR INCORRECT?*   If the sentence is correct, write a "C" on the line provided. If not, write an "I" for incorrect, then REWRITE the sentence to make it correct. You can change any part of the sentence to make it correct.

1. Carl was studying the <u>demography</u> of the state, so he investigated the variety of plants and animals in the area.

   I  _____

2. In the study of <u>graphology</u> large looping letters indicate a different personality type than small tight letters.

   C  _____

3. It is important to wash your hands often so that you do not <u>transmit</u> germs to others.

   C  _____

4. The forest experienced a <u>transformation</u> through the years of being left in its natural state.

   I  _____

5. The two-year-old experienced <u>autonomy</u> when his mother put him to bed against his wishes.

   I  _____

6. My <u>transient</u> sister lived in the same house and had the same job for 20 years.

   I  _____

7. Jim wrote an <u>autobiography</u> about his favorite football coach.

8. I was lucky to attend an <u>autograph</u> session where several sports players signed their pictures.

---

*SHORT ANSWER*    Write your answers on a separate sheet of paper.

1. Pretend you are thinking about moving. What information about the <u>demography</u> of the area would you want to know?

2. Research <u>graphology</u> on the Internet. Use what you find to analyze your handwriting and that of a friend's.

3. What can you do so that you do not <u>transmit</u> a virus through your email?

4. List three things that would give your house, apartment, or dorm room a <u>transformation</u>.

5. List three areas in your life in which you have <u>autonomy</u>.

6. If you had a <u>transient</u> lifestyle, what three things would you decide to carry with you all the time?

7. List three people whose <u>autographs</u> you either already have or would like to have.

8. If you were writing your <u>autobiography,</u> what three events or people that influenced your life would you write about?

# Power Words

1. **annotate**   ăn'ō-tāt'   verb

   To finish a literary work with critical commentary; explanatory notes

   After reading the sociology chapter, Alicia began to **annotate** each section with *margin notes* so that she would have a thorough understanding of the concepts.

2. **introvert**   ĭn'trə-vûrt'   noun/verb

   (verb) To direct or turn something inward or in on itself

   Jonathan **introverted** his feelings of enthusiasm for his recent job promotion and *did not share them* when he found out that his brother had lost his job.

   (noun) A person who tends to shrink from social contacts and to become preoccupied with his or her own thoughts

   Alana was very *shy and reserved*. She was a true **introvert** when it came to social activities.

   **Synonym:** loner

3. **extrovert**   ĕk'strə-vûrt'   noun

   A person concerned more with practical realities than with inner thoughts and feelings

   Stacey and Eric were extreme **extroverts**. They both *enjoyed social activities* that involved getting together with friends or coworkers every weekend.

   **Synonym:** gregarious

4. **paraphrase**   păr'ə-frāz'   verb

   A restatement of a text or passage in another form or other words; a restatement of text or passage material in one's own words

   Bret tried to **paraphrase** the *information that his professor gave about the test to his roommate*, but, unfortunately, he left out the most important part—the due date.

*Practice Exercises*

1. Practice <u>annotation</u> in one of your content textbooks. Use the following steps:

   • Read a paragraph.

   • Determine the most important information that you need to know.

   • Paraphrase the information into your own words.

   • Write a few key words or phrases in the margin.

   • After you are done with a section, go back and review your annotations.

2. Describe a preferred study environment for an <u>extrovert</u> and an <u>introvert</u>. What might be the differences in their preferences?

3. Go back to one of the Dictionary sections in this chapter and <u>paraphrase</u> the definitions.

# Chapter Review

*Extend Your Learning*

Use one or more of the following exercises to practice the words in this chapter. Remember that it is important to use a variety of strategies in order to maximize your learning.

   • Using Part A words, draw an outline of a foot (*ped-*) and a stick figure of a child (*ped-*). Write the words from Part A in the appropriate figure. For Part B words, make a simple drawing to illustrate the meaning of the words with the word part *trans-*.

   • Write new sentences using the words in this chapter. Do your thinking out loud and write the sentences only after your have perfected them.

   • Write new sentences using words from this chapter. Use the information that you learned about context clues in Chapters Three and Four and include context clues in your sentences so that the meaning of each word is clear.

   • Write the words on index cards—one word per card. Mix them up and then reorder them into groups according to the structural elements. Next, develop sentences using as many words as you can in one sentence. As you do this, put those word cards that you used into one pile; continue the process until all the word cards are used.

*Expanded Word Forms*

Select the appropriate word form for each of the sentences.

| transmit | transmitted | transmitting | demography | demographics |
|----------|-------------|--------------|------------|--------------|
| annotates | annotating | annotated | annotations | |

1. The _____ that Megan made while reading her psychology textbook helped her tremendously on the exam. By _____ the text, she was able to focus on the most important elements of the chapters. When her roommate asked how she _____ the chapter, she described in detail the process that she used. Megan told her that when she _____ she understands and remembers what she reads.

2. Joe studied the _____ of three different locations before deciding where to look for a job. Some of the _____ he considered were age of the population, where most people worked, and the average income.

3. Please _____ all of your papers through the university's email system, not to my personal email account.

4. Jillian _____ her final paper to her professor by email two weeks early because she was called to active military duty. By _____ it early, she did not lose any points for the paper.

*Puzzle Fun*

**Across**

4. an object that is supported by "feet"
6. to convey or send
9. a signature
11. one who cares for the feet
12. like the census
16. not permanent
17. shy; loner
18. a lover of technology

**Down**

1. lover of books
2. child molester
3. a change usually for the better
5. self-governing or ruling
7. to make explanatory notes
8. social; gregarious
10. relating to children
13. a lectern
14. the art of analyzing one's writing
15. the art of teaching
19. restate

# CHAPTER NINE

# Preparation: The Key to Success

*Before anything else, preparation is the key to success.*

Alexander Graham Bell (1847–1922)

---

## CHAPTER OBJECTIVE

**Students will be able to identify and use words with the following common structural elements:**

Roots: soph, spec, cogn
Prefixes: contr-, counter-, anti-
Suffix: -ency

---

## CHAPTER OUTLINE

 **Memory Tip**   Memory Games

 **Learning Strategy**   Recitation

**Part A**
*Words to Learn*

controversy          sophomore
counterpart          philosophy
contraband           antisocial
counterproductive    antiestablishment
sophisticated

*Structural Elements*

contr-               counter-
soph                 anti-

**Part B**
*Words to Learn*

cognitive            spectacular
incognito            spectacle
metacognition        urgency
speculate            agency

*Structural Elements*

cogn                 spec
-ency

*Power Words*

manipulate

manual

ubiquitous

## 💡 *Memory Tip*   Memory Games

Learning is not always work—you can turn your vocabulary learning into a game. The following game will help you train your brain to recall items or information:

Have someone fill a tray with 20 random items. While studying the items, create a story in your mind using all of the items. It's okay if your story is silly and does not make sense; just use your imagination to visualize the story in your head. Cover the tray, write your story down, and see how many of the objects you can recall. This same story memory game can be used with a list of vocabulary words or facts you must memorize for class.

Here are two interesting websites to help you play games and improve your memory:

- http://www.ehow.com/info_8416645_memory-games-college-students.html#ixzz1jGPkD96J

- http://www.improvememory.org/games

## 🔍 *Learning Strategy*   Recitation—Restating in Your Own Words from Memory

To truly understand what you are learning, you need to be able to restate the information in your own words from memory. It is not enough to memorize your notes or the textbook. In most cases you will need to be able to apply what you are learning to different situations. For example, with these words you are learning you need to understand them in different sentences and in different variations. Another example is in a psychology course where you will be asked to relate what you are learning to examples and situations different from those presented in class.

You can use recitation when studying by:

Making study cards and testing yourself as you go through them (Hint: Be sure to mix them up so you are learning them in different orders.)

Practicing using new vocabulary words in different sentences and different forms

Explaining the definitions to a friend

Teaching someone else

When studying your notes, covering the page and restating what you just reviewed

Same for reading your textbooks—after completing a section, closing your book and restating what you just read

## Part A

🗨 *WORDS TO LEARN—SEE AND SAY*   Use the pronunciation guide on the first page of this book to help you SAY each word.

1. controversy          kŏn′trə-vûr′sē
2. counterpart          koun′tər-pärt′
3. counterproductive    koun′tər-prə-dŭk′tĭv
4. contraband           kŏn′trə-bănd′
5. sophisticated        sə-fĭs′tĭ-kā′tĭd
6. sophomore            sŏf′ə-môr′
7. philosophy           fĭ-lŏs′ə-fē
8. antisocial           ăn′tē-sō′shəl
9. antiestablishment    ăn′tē-ĭ-stăb′lĭsh-mənt

*STRUCTURAL ELEMENTS*   Look at the structural elements of each word. Use these elements to unlock the word's meaning.

| | |
|---|---|
| contr-, counter- | against, opposite |
| soph | wise, wisdom |
| anti- | against or opposite |

 *CONTEXT CLUES*   Read the sentences. Use the words around the unfamiliar word to determine the word's meaning. Words in bold are the vocabulary words; words in italic are the context clues.

1. The **controversy** *between the professor and the student* resulted in a meeting with the president of the college followed by a suspension for the student.

2. The president of XYZ company called his **counterpart**, the *president of ABC company*, for advice.

3. The school has an extensive list of items that are considered **contraband**; any student, faculty, or staff *who possesses these items will be banned from the school.*

4. It is **counterproductive** to *wash the dishes after* they have been through the dishwasher.

5. High school math is much more **sophisticated** *and advanced* than elementary school math.

6. The **sophomore** believed he knew all of the rules and had all of the answers. It took him several months to realize that he was *just a beginner in the search for wisdom and understanding.*

7. *Plato, Aristotle*, and other Greek **philosophers** contributed greatly to our understanding of the nature of reality and existence and of what it is possible to know.

8. Someone exhibiting **antisocial** behavior *does not relate well to others in a social setting.*

9. Because Joey was *against the traditional ways of governing*, he joined the **antiestablishment** party.

 *DICTIONARY*   Read the following definitions.

1. controversy   noun

   **Etymology:** contr[o] (opposite or against) ver (turn)

   A dispute, especially a public one, between sides holding opposing views

   The **controversy** *between the CFO and the CEO caused the company's stock to drop rapidly.*

   **Synonyms:** debate, difference

   **Antonym:** agreement

2. counterpart   noun

   **Etymology:** counter (opposite or against) part (part)

   One that closely resembles another; one that has the same functions and characteristics as another; a corresponding person or thing

   England's *prime minister* is the **counterpart** of the United States' *secretary of state.*

   **Vocabulary Tip:** You are probably wondering why *counterpart* has the structural element *counter* (meaning opposite) when the definition is someone who does the *same* thing. The answer is simple-a counterpart does the same thing as someone or something in an *opposite* company or place.

3. contraband   noun

   **Etymology:** contra (opposite or against) band (legal proclamation)

   Goods prohibited by law or treaty from being imported or exported

   With the recent war on terrorism, airlines have identified many common items as **contraband** and *refused to let them be taken on a plane.*

4. **counterproductive**   adjective

   **Etymology:** counter (against or opposite) productive (producing something)

   Tending to hinder rather than serve one's purpose or goal

   It is **counterproductive** to spend money on *gambling and then have to work overtime to make up* for the losses.

   **Synonym:** harmful

5. **sophisticated**   adjective

   **Etymology:** soph (wise or wisdom)

   Having acquired worldly knowledge or refinement; complex

   *At the age of 15*, it was *difficult to view* Jenna as being **sophisticated**.

   **Synonyms:** cosmopolitan, worldly wise

   **Antonym:** naive

6. **sophomore**   noun

   **Etymology:** sopho (wise or wisdom) more (moron)

   A second-year student; one who is immature or superficial

   The **sophomore** was able to offer little to the understanding of how to produce detailed, documented research because the research course was not required *until the junior year.*

   **Synonym:** immature

   **Vocabulary Tip:** This word—*sophomore*—refers to someone who has little life experience. A sophomore in high school or college still has two more years in which to grow and learn.

7. **philosophy**   noun

   **Etymology:** philo (love) soph (wise or wisdom)

   The science dealing with the general causes and principles of things; study of fundamental beliefs

   Most teachers have the same **philosophpy,** *or beliefs about teaching*: to serve their students with the most respect, concern, and passion for knowledge.

   **Synonyms:** principles, doctrine

8. **antisocial**   adjective

   **Etymology:** anti (against or opposite) social (being with others)

   Shunning the company of others; not social; marked by behavior that violates accepted social customs

   Gangs engaging in *vandalism and other* **antisocial** *behavior* have caused many problems for urban areas.

   **Synonyms:** aloof, standoffish

   **Antonyms:** cordial, sociable

9. **antiestablishment**   adjective

   **Etymology:** anti (against or opposite) establishment (the controlling group)

   Marked by opposition or hostility to conventional social, political, or economic values or principles

   The **antiestablishment** candidates promised to *disband the army, Congress, and the cabinet if elected.*

## Practice Exercises

### MULTIPLE CHOICE

1. Which of the following would *not* cause a <u>controversy</u> between a parent and a teenager?
   a. what time to come home on the weekends ✓
   b. how much allowance he or she should receive
   c. what flavor of ice cream to have for dessert
   d. when he or she can start to date

2. Which of the following would be your <u>counterpart</u>?
   a. someone who has completely different tastes in music
   b. someone going to college at either a two- or a four-year institution ✓
   c. someone nearing retirement age
   d. the CEO of the local bank

3. Which of the following is an antonym for <u>contraband</u>?
   a. banned
   b. forbidden ✓
   c. unlawful
   d. legal

4. Which of the following is an example of a <u>counterproductive</u> activity?
   a. buying a latte every day when you are trying to save money ✓
   b. buying a new car when you get a job an hour away from home
   c. sending your mother flowers on her birthday
   d. talking to your professor when you know that you will miss class

5. Which situation would most likely appeal to a <u>sophisticated</u> person?
   a. eating at McDonald's ✓
   b. attending a drag race
   c. going to a go-cart track and racing his or her neighbors
   d. attending a lecture on eighteenth-century art

6. Which is an example of <u>sophomoric</u> behavior?
   a. throwing water balloons out a hotel window ✓
   b. holding the door for a young woman with a baby stroller
   c. knowing when to clap at a concert
   d. not talking while watching a movie in a theater

7. What does a <u>philosopher</u> probably like to do?
   a. think about serious life issues that impact most people ✓
   b. investigate the equipment necessary for off-road racing
   c. discuss the merits of McDonald's versus Wendy's
   d. play "Go Fish" with several other philosophers

8. Where would you most likely find an <u>antisocial</u> person?
   a. going to a concert with a group of friends
   b. campaigning for local office ✓
   c. eating at the community table in the school cafeteria
   d. having coffee alone at Starbucks

9. An <u>antiestablishment</u> candidate most likely would
   a. pledge to keep things the way they are ✗
   b. align himself or herself with the current government officials
   c. tell the voters what is wrong with the way things are currently run
   d. not offer any ideas for change

*FILL IN THE BLANK*   Select the BEST word for each sentence. Use each word only once.

controversy ⑦     counterpart ⑧     counterproductive ⑨     contraband ①
sophisticated ③     sophomore ⑤     philosophy ⑥     antisocial ②
antiestablishment ④

1. Joel was arrested when the border agents found _____ hidden in his luggage.

2. Even though Rosalie was _____, she made an effort to make friends and eat with other people for lunch.

3. Sue wanted to be _____, but when she went to the expensive restaurant she did not know which fork to use.

4. Jim ran on a(n) _____ platform, promising to make changes in every aspect of how the fraternity was organized.

5. The freshman hoped to complete enough credits to be a _____ next semester.

6. The _____ major studied the basic beliefs about life and death.

7. The football game ended with a _____ because of the questionable call by the officials.

8. My _____ in the other sorority held the same office that I did.

9. It was _____ for Sam to withdraw from several classes when he hoped to graduate in four years.

*CORRECT OR INCORRECT?*   If the sentence is correct, write a "C" on the line provided. If not, write an "I" for incorrect, then REWRITE the sentence to make it correct. You can change any part of the sentence to make it correct.

1. The college president's decision caused so much <u>controversy</u> among the faculty and staff that everyone agreed to work together to accomplish the goals.
   I _____

2. Dale's <u>counterpart</u> in the new company held a job that was the opposite of his.
   I _____

3. Sam was embarrassed when the <u>contraband</u> perfume he gave Susie for her birthday was seized by the border agents.
   C _____

4. Greg was very successful in his new position in the company because he took advantage of every <u>counter-productive</u> opportunity that he could find.
   I _____

5. The mathematical proof was so <u>sophisticated</u> that even the youngest and least knowledgeable student was able to understand it.
   I _____

6. The college student was embarrassed by his friends' <u>sophomoric</u> behavior.
   C _____

7. The <u>antisocial</u> student was always surrounded by friends.
   I _____

8. Jeremy grew up in a home that was quite <u>antiestablishment</u>; his family refused to follow most of the township's regulations regarding burning and recycling.
   C _____

9. The <u>philosopher</u> spent all of her time studying plants that grew in the farthest reaches of the Antarctic.
   I _____

*SHORT ANSWER*   Write your answers on a separate sheet of paper.

1. Describe a situation in a college dormitory that could cause a <u>controversy</u>.

2. Name an item that is considered <u>contraband</u> when currently traveling by air. Why is it classified that way?

3. What three words would describe your <u>counterpart</u> in another family or studying at another school?

4. Take a minute to reflect on your academic career. What is one or more <u>counterproductive</u> activities that you do that, if changed, would help you be more successful? Why?

5. How would someone act at a formal dinner if he or she were <u>sophisticated</u>? Unsophisticated?

6. What are the requirements at your institution to be a <u>sophomore</u>?

7. What is something a <u>philosopher</u> might think about?

8. What are three activites an <u>antisocial</u> person probably would like? What are three that that person probably would not like?

9. If you were an <u>antiestablishment</u> candidate for office at your school, what three things would you change?

# Part B

   *WORDS TO LEARN—SEE AND SAY*   Use the pronunciation guide on the first page of this book to help you SAY each word.

1. cognitive         kŏg′nĭ-tĭv

2. incognito         ĭn′kŏg-nē′tō

3. metacognition     mĕt-ə kŏg-nĭsh′ən

4. speculate         spĕk′yə-lāt′

5. spectacular       spĕk-tăk′yə-lər

6. spectacle         spĕk′tə-kəl

7. urgency           ûr′jən-sē

8. agency            ā′jən-sē

   *STRUCTURAL ELEMENTS*   Look at the structural elements of each word. Use these elements to unlock the word's meaning.

| | |
|---|---|
| spec | to view, to see |
| cogn | know, knowledge |
| -ency | state or quality of |

   *CONTEXT CLUES*   Read the sentences. Use the words around the unfamiliar word to determine word's meaning. Words in bold are the vocabulary words; words in italic are the context clues.

1. Children begin to develop **cognitive** abilities to *listen and respond* to directions before entering kindergarten.

2. The mother went to her teenager's party **incognito**—*no one recognized her* with the long blonde wig and cowboy boots.

3. Dr. Jones encouraged his students to use their **metacognitive** abilities as they *examined how well they each understood his lecture.*

4. Jack **speculated** on the *risky new business* in the hope that he would make a lot of money.

5. The view was so **spectacular** that it *took my breath away.*

6. Don't make a **spectacle** of yourself and *draw attention to* improper behavior.

7. The messenger's **urgency** to deliver the letter was apparent because of *how quickly* he ran up the steps and *how loudly* he knocked on the door.

8. I made an appointment to work with someone at the employment **agency** because her *business is to know* what jobs are available that would match my skills.

 *DICTIONARY* Read the following definitions.

1. **cognitive** adjective

   **Etymology:** cogni (knowledge, thinking, understanding) -tive (relating to the act of)

   Relating to knowledge or perception; referring to the ability to acquire knowledge

   The school psychologist was determined to help the young child develop the necessary **cognitive skills** in order *to be passed on to the next grade.*

   **Synonym:** intellectual

   **Antonyms:** emotional, intuitive

2. **incognito** adjective/adverb

   **Etymology:** in (not) cogn (knowledge or knowing) ito (little)

   (adjective/adverb) With one's identity disguised or concealed

   Espionage, or spying, requires that you are artful in developing ways of going into public areas **incognito** *so that you are not recognized.*

   **Synonyms:** disguised, hidden

   **Antonyms:** revealed, exposed

3. **metacognition** noun

   **Etymology:** meta (big, transcending) cogn (knowldege, thinking, knowing) -tion (state, act or condition of)

   The act of thinking about thinking; understanding how one thinks

   When discussing your thinking or understanding, it is understood that you are using **metacognition** to try *to explain your thinking.*

4. **speculate** verb

   **Etymology:** spec (view or see) ate (to make or cause to be)

   To think or reason on inconclusive evidence; to assume to be true without conclusive evidence

   *Without performing any blood tests,* the doctor **speculated** that high cholesterol was a contributing factor to the patient's health problems.

5. **spectacular** adjective

   **Etymology:** spec[t] (see or view) -ar (adjective form relates to)

   Relates to something that is impressive or sensational

   The **spectacular** fireworks display drew many *"ohs"* and *"ahs"* from the crowd.

   **Synonym:** fantastic

   **Antonyms:** boring, bland

6. spectacle   noun

   **Etymology:** spec (see or view)

   Something that is remarkable or impressive to see (usually in a negative way)

   The coeds made a **spectacle** of themselves at the fraternity party by *throwing their shoes and other articles of clothing into the pool.*

   **Synonym:** show-off

   **Antonym:** ordinariness; normalcy

7. urgency   noun

   **Etymology:** urgere (press or drive) ency (state or quality of)

   The quality or condition of being very important

   It is always important to heed the tornado *warnings* because they will *identify* the **urgency** of the situation.

   **Synonym:** importance

8. agency   noun

   **Etymology:** agere (establishment where something is done for another) ency (state or quality of)

   A business or other institution that is given permission to act for others; given to a particular function

   The *CIA* is an **agency** that most people recognize. It is often mentioned in spy movies when the hero needs information from the *Central Intelligence Agency.*

   **Synonyms:** bureau, authority

## *Practice Exercises*

### *MULTIPLE CHOICE*

1. The spy was <u>incognito</u> so that
   a. he could change his clothes quickly without being noticed
   b. no one could identify him as he entered the room
   c. he looked different than everyone else
   d. the person in charge could identify him easily

2. <u>Cognitive</u> ability relates to which of the following?
   a. the number of sit-ups you can do
   b. how fast you can order and eat your dinner
   c. getting a good night's sleep
   d. how well you can remember the dates in history

3. What would you think about if you were practicing <u>metacognition</u>?
   a. what you want to have for dinner
   b. what to wear to the concert Friday night
   c. how well you understand the math homework
   d. what grade you earned on yesterday's math quiz

4. Which of the following activities is an example of <u>speculating</u>?
   a. stopping for coffee at Starbucks
   b. choosing a major without doing any research
   c. deciding which movie to see
   d. saving money to buy a new car

5. Which of the following could be <u>spectacular</u>?
   a. doing your laundry on Saturday night
   b. the first time you see the Statue of Liberty
   c. earning a C on an exam when you expected an A
   d. remembering to wash your hands for 20 seconds before eating lunch

6. What do you do if you make a <u>spectacle</u> of yourself at a party?
   a. Act calmly and politely.
   b. Talk to several people and leave early.
   c. Act silly and make everyone look at you.
   d. Help the host clean up afterward.

7. Which of the following words means the same as <u>urgency</u>?
   a. eccentric, unique
   b. importance, time-sensitivity
   c. complacent, casual
   d. superfluous, impetuous

8. You would seek help at the XYZ <u>Agency</u> because
   a. it has the knowledge to help in the area you want
   b. you like its name
   c. your best friend works there
   d. you have nothing better to do

*FILL IN THE BLANK*   Select the BEST word for each sentence. Use each word only once.

cognitive   incognito   metacognition   urgency
speculated   spectacular   spectacle   agency

1. As a teacher I think it is important to help my students think about their _____ so that they understand how they learn.

2. The entire second-grade class enjoyed the _____ created when a dog got into the school and the principal chased it down the hall.

3. Wally lost all of his money when he _____ on a business opportunity he read about on the Internet and that turned out to be a scam.

4. Actors and actresses often will go out in public _____ to avoid being bombarded by enthusiastic fans.

5. The view was so _____ that Marjie just stood and looked for a long time.

6. Dr. Black was praising Jim's _____ ability when he said Jim was a fast learner.

7. The manager tried to explain the _____ of the situation to his staff. They had to complete the project within the week or the company would not get paid.

8. Sam went to the Small Business _____, or bureau, for advice when he wanted to start his own cleaning company.

*CORRECT OR INCORRECT?*   If the sentence is correct, write a "C" on the line provided. It not, write an "I" for incorrect, then REWRITE the sentence to make it correct. You can change any part of the sentence to make it correct.

1. My <u>metacognitive</u> abilities helped me when it came time to buy a new car.
   _____

2. Because he was <u>incognito</u>, the spy was easy to identify in the crowd of diplomats.
   _____

3. Learning a foreign language does not require any <u>cognitive</u> ability.

_____

4. Julie always made very quick decisions and often carefully <u>speculated</u> on what to do next.

_____

5. Carol was a <u>spectacular</u> hostess. The food was burnt, the coffee was cold, and everyone went home early.

_____

6. The <u>spectacle</u> created by the quiet young child entertained everyone on the bus.

_____

7. Because of the <u>urgency</u> of the situation, everyone worked slowly and took many breaks.

_____

8. The ABC <u>Agency</u> was a group of friends who met every Wednesday for coffee.

_____

*SHORT ANSWER*   Write your answers on a separate sheet of paper.

1. What three things have you done today that required <u>cognitive</u> ability?
2. When and where would you find people dressed <u>incognito</u>?
3. Name three times you have used <u>metacognition</u> in the past week.
4. What decisions in life should you consider carefully instead of <u>speculating</u> on?
5. Name three events or experiences from your life that you consider to be <u>spectacular</u>. Explain.
6. What is one <u>spectacle</u> that you caused in your childhood?
7. Describe three situations in college in which you feel a sense of <u>urgency</u>.
8. Name three <u>agencies</u> in your local area and describe what they do.

## Power Words

1. **manipulate**   mə-nĭp′yə-lāt′   verb

   To move or control by hand or by mechanical means, especially in a skillful manner

   When teaching young children mathematics, it is important to provide them with *blocks or other objects* that they can **manipulate.**

   To influence or manage shrewdly or deviously

   Even though Maggie was only eight years old, she was able to **manipulate** *her parents into giving her whatever she wanted.*

   **Synonyms:** handle, exploit

2. **manual**   măn′yōō-əl   adjective/noun

   (adjective) Done by, used by, or operated with the hands; employing human rather than mechanical labor

   **Manual** dexterity is one of the requirements for the small appliance repairperson position because the employee will be *using his or her hands* to repair small items.

   (noun) A small reference book, especially one giving instructions

   New cars come with an owner's **manual** that is required *reading in order to understand how all of the controls function.*

3. **ubiquitous**  yo͞o-bĭk′wĭ-təs  adjective

   Being or seeming to be everywhere at the same time

   Political signs are **ubiquitous** right before any election; *they are on every street corner.*

   **Synonyms:** omnipresent, widespread

   **Antonyms:** rare, seldom

## *Practice Exercises*

1.  Write a paragraph describing the differences between driving a car with an automatic transmission and one with a standard transmission. In your description, use the words <u>manipulate</u> and <u>manual</u>.

2.  Name two things that are <u>ubiquitous</u> at your school.

# Chapter Review
## *Extend Your Learning*

Use one or more of the following exercises to practice the words in this chapter. Remember that it is important to use a variety of strategies in order to maximize your learning.

- Construct word webs to help you learn the words in this chapter. Expand your web with additional words containing the same word elements.

- Play your favorite music at the same time you review the words and their definitions. After you are done, try to remember the definition for each word while listening to the same music.

- Using your knowledge of word parts, find other words with the same part. Make a list of the new words and their definitions.

- Find an empty classroom where you can use the chalkboard or whiteboard. On the board construct word webs to help you learn the words in this chapter. Expand your web with additional words containing the same word elements.

## *Expanded Word Forms*

Select the appropriate word form for each of the sentences.

| | | | | |
|---|---|---|---|---|
| philosophy | philosophical | manual | manually | manipulate |
| speculate | spectacular | speculated | controversy | controversial |

1. The investor _____ on an unknown stock. He hoped to make a _____ profit, but unfortunately the company closed and he lost everything. In the future he will do more research and not _____ on the unknown.

2. When studying to be a teacher it is important to begin to develop a _____ of teaching. This _____ perspective will help you when deciding on the approach that you will take with your class.

3. Many subjects are very _____ in college classrooms, but it is important to understand the _____ may exist so that you can defend or reject a point of view.

4. It is important to read your car's _____ when you get a new vehicle. Some cars shift gears _____ whereas others are totally automatic. You must be aware of how to _____ all of the controls in your new vehicle before taking it out on the highway.

*Puzzle Fun*

**Across**

5. immature
6. without full evidence
7. relating to doing without the aid of machinery, basically doing by hand
8. science dealing with principles or doctrines
9. tending to hinder rather than help
10. prohibited goods

**Down**

1. thinking about thinking
2. in opposition to the conventional wisdom of something
3. one that corresponds to
4. intellectual

# CHAPTER TEN
# Words: The Beginning, Not the End

*Always bear in mind that your own resolution to succeed is more important than any other one thing.*

Abraham Lincoln, 1809–1865, 16th President of the United States

## CHAPTER OBJECTIVE

**Students will be able to identify and use words with the following common structural elements:**

Roots: log, loq
Prefixes: mal-, bene-, eu-, re-

## CHAPTER OUTLINE

 **Memory Tip**   Using Multiple Senses to Aid Memory

 **Learning Strategy**   Your Learning Environment

**Part A**
*Words to Learn*

| | |
|---|---|
| benediction | malefactor |
| benefactor | malediction |
| benevolent | eulogy |
| benign | euphemism |
| malign | |

*Structural Elements*

| | |
|---|---|
| mal- | eu- |
| bene- | |

**Part B**
*Words to Learn*

| | |
|---|---|
| loquacious | repudiate |
| retract | revelation |
| repercussion | dialogue |
| relinquish | logophile |

*Structural Elements*

| | |
|---|---|
| re- | log, loq |

*Power Words*

| | |
|---|---|
| eradicate | decimate |

**117**

## 💡 *Memory Tip*   Using Multiple Senses to Aid Memory

We have five senses: vision, hearing, touch, smell, and taste. In Chapter One we defined learning as using varied and repeated strategies over time. The more senses you can involve in your studying, the more successfully you will remember the information. Review the ideas in Chapter One. What can you add? Here are some more ideas:

- *Vision:* Draw a picture to depict the new words or information.
- *Hearing:* Sing the information you need to learn to a rap beat or in rhyme form.
- *Touch:* Manipulate your study cards; use a favorite pen or pencil.
- *Smell:* Light a scented candle when studying.
- *Taste:* Eat peppermint candy while studying and then the same type of candy while taking the exam.

## 🔍 *Learning Strategy*   Your Leaning Environment

*Where* you study is as important as *how* you study. Eliminate as many distractions as possible so that you can focus. Here are some ideas:

- Turn off the TV, email, Facebook, etc.
- If you are going to study with friends, make sure they also are serious about their work and won't tempt you to socialize.
- Go to the library instead of your room or apartment.
- If you are going to study at home, have a designated place (not your bed!) where your mind will be on learning.

## Part A

🗨 *WORDS TO LEARN—SEE AND SAY*   Use the pronunciation guide on the first page of this book to help you SAY each word.

| | | |
|---|---|---|
| 1. | benediction | bĕn′ĭ-dĭk′shən |
| 2. | benefactor | bĕn′ə-făk′tər |
| 3. | benevolent | bə-nĕv′ə-lənt |
| 4. | benign | bĭ-nīn′ |
| 5. | malign | mə-līn′ |
| 6. | malefactor | măl′ə-făk′tər |
| 7. | malediction | măl′ĭ-dĭk′shən |
| 8. | eulogy | yoo′lə-jē |
| 9. | euphemism | yoo′fə-mĭz′əm |

 *STRUCTURAL ELEMENTS*   Look at the structural elements of each word. Use these elements to unlock the word's meaning.

| | |
|---|---|
| mal- | bad |
| bene- | good |
| eu- | good |

*CONTEXT CLUES*   Read the sentences. Use the words around the unfamiliar word to determine the word's meaning. Words in bold are the vocabulary words; words in italic are the context clues.

1. The **benediction** that was *spoken at the end of the awards banquet* was an inspiration to all who attended.

2. Bill and Melinda Gates, the **benefactors** of the Bill and Melinda Gates Foundation, with a *$29 billion endowment,* have surpassed the World Health Organization as top global funder for health issues including HIV, malaria, and tuberculosis research.

3. Chuck was regarded by all who knew him as a **benevolent** man—he was *always helping someone* less fortunate than him.

4. The FDA has indicated that the meat and milk products produced from cloned animals are **benign** to the environment and the consumer; therefore, it *may approve* the sale of cloned meat products very soon.

5. Never **malign** your friends or they *won't be your friends* for long.

6. The **malefactor** was apprehended and sentenced to jail for *his crimes.*

7. After years of trying to overcome the spiteful **maledictions** of its competitors, Blue Note, Inc. had to succumb to the *ill words* and declare bankruptcy.

8. The **eulogy** *written by the deceased's brother* was very heartfelt.

9. Most people will try to use a **euphemism** *in place of a word that might be insulting or hurtful.*

 *DICTIONARY*   Read the following definitions.

1. benediction   noun

   **Etymology:** bene (good) dict (speak or say) tion (condition of)

   A blessing; an expression of good wishes

   The senior class president offered a *heartwarming* **benediction** at the senior banquet.

   **Synonyms:** prayer, invocation

2. benefactor   noun

   **Etymology:** bene (good) fact (make) or (something or someone who)

   One that gives aid, especially financial aid

   Mr. Jones is a noted **benefactor** to the community; he has *sponsored the education of three young people* each year for the past ten years.

   **Synonyms:** supporter, donor

   **Antonym:** beneficiary

3. benevolent   adjective

   **Etymology:** bene (good) volens (to wish)

   Characterized by or suggestive of doing good

   He was a **benevolent** man, determined to do what he could to *make life easier and happier* for others.

   **Synonym:** charitable

   **Antonyms:** malevolent, evil

4. benign   adjective

   **Etymology:** bene (good)

   Of a kind and gentle disposition; of no danger to health

   Valerie's **benign,** *nonthreatening,* manner made all of her coworkers feel comfortable.

**Synonym:** harmless

**Anonyms:** malignant, harmful

5. malign    verb/adjective

**Etymology:** mal (bad)

(verb) To make evil, harmful, and often untrue statements about; speak evil of

Jacob was accused of **maligning** his previous employer by *spreading vicious gossip* after he had been fired from the job.

(adjective) Evil in disposition, nature, or intent; having or showing malice or ill will

Andrew's **malign** *nature made it very difficult for anyone to remain his friend.*

**Synonyms:** hurtful, deleterious

**Antonym:** praise

**Vocabulary Tip:** When someone maligns another person in speech or writing, the damaging things said are often untrue.

6. malefactor    noun

**Etymology:** mal (bad) fact (make) or (someone or something that)

One that has committed a crime

It is very important that the police unit protects the citizens from the *evil* **malefactors** who lurk in the community.

**Synonyms:** criminal, evildoer

**Antonyms:** humanitarian, hero, benefactor

7. malediction    noun

**Etymology:** mal (bad) dict (speak or say)

Slander; curse; evil statement directed at someone else

*Calling someone a "jerk" or an "idiot" is an example* of a **malediction**.

**Synonyms:** curse, condemnation

8. eulogy    noun

**Etymology:** eu (good) log (words)

A positive speech or written tribute, especially praising someone who has died

The **eulogy** *delivered at the funeral was inspiring and comforting* to the family who recently lost their beloved son.

**Synonyms:** praise, tribute

**Antonyms:** defamation, malediction

9. euphemism    noun

**Etymology:** eu (good) pheme (speech)

A word or expression that people use when they want to talk about something unpleasant or embarrassing without mentioning the thing itself

Many politicians use **euphemisms** *such as "homeland security"* instead of "antiterrorism" to provide a sense of control and comfort.

**Vocabulary Tip:** A euphemism is more than just an understatement. It is a word or description used to be more politically correct or to be more sensitive.

*Practice Exercises*

*MULTIPLE CHOICE*

1. A <u>benign</u> statement is
   a. malevolent
   b. harmless
   c. threatening
   d. earth-shattering

2. An antonym for <u>benediction</u> is
   a. prayer
   b. thanksgiving
   c. malediction
   d. blessing

3. How would you describe someone who is <u>benevolent</u>?
   a. She thinks only about herself.
   b. She thinks of others before herself.
   c. She always puts herself first.
   d. She has a generous benefactor who has given her many gifts.

4. Which of the following would be done by a <u>benefactor</u>?
   a. fund a college scholarship
   b. overcharge a customer at a restaurant
   c. receive an annonymous gift
   d. inherit money from his or her great aunt

5. Which of the following would describe a <u>malefactor</u>?
   a. generous with his time and money
   b. innocent
   c. guilty of several crimes
   d. a leader in the community

6. Which of the following is an example of a <u>malediction</u>?
   a. "You are great."
   b. "You are a jerk."
   c. "You are exceptional."
   d. "You are spectacular."

7. When you <u>malign</u> someone you
   a. say something negative about him or her
   b. say something positive about him or her
   c. refute what someone has said about him or her
   d. turn him or her in to the police

8. Which of the following words would you expect to hear in a <u>eulogy</u>?
   a. mean, evil
   b. self-serving
   c. stingy
   d. generous, kindhearted

9. A <u>euphemism</u> for garbage collector could be
   a. dumpster diver
   b. sanitation engineer
   c. garage sale addict
   d. pickup artist

*FILL IN THE BLANK*   Select the BEST word for each sentence. Use each word only once.

| | | | | |
|---|---|---|---|---|
| benign | benediction | benefactor | benevolent | maligned |
| maledictions | malefactor | euphemism | eulogy | |

1. The priest knew the deceased well, so the _____ was very personal and moving.

2. The anonymous _____ gave the school money to finance three cultural performances in the next semester.

3. The visiting pastor was invited to give the _____ at the end of the service.

4. The _____ guard dog was useless; he never barked at strangers.

5. The actress sued the entertainment newspaper because she felt she had been _____ in an article it published.

6. As the teacher entered the room, she heard numerous students speaking _____ that were not appropriate behavior in school; therefore, she called the principal.

7. The _____ was apprehended after he used the money stolen from the bank to buy an airplane ticket out of the country.

8. Instead of using the word *stupid* to describe my friend's dog, I tried to find a _____ that didn't sound quite so bad.

9. Because I want to be remembered as a _____ person, I give money to many charities and volunteer my time for others.


*CORRECT OR INCORRECT?*   If the sentence is correct, write a "C" on the line provided. If not, write an "I" for incorrect, then REWRITE the sentence to make it correct. You can change any part of the sentence to make it correct.

1. The student government president opened the meeting with a <u>benediction</u>.

   _____

2. Joe's chance of recovery was excellent because the tumor was <u>benign</u>.

   _____

3. Due to the <u>benefactor</u>'s help, the charitable organization had to file for bankruptcy.

   _____

4. The police officer was feeling <u>benevolent</u> when he did not give Joe a speeding ticket.

   _____

5. Because of the <u>maligned</u> nature of his crimes, the criminal was sentenced to life in prison.

   _____

6. The <u>malefactor</u> was praised by a memorable <u>eulogy</u> at his funeral.

   _____

7. Sue was pleased by all the <u>maledictions</u> that she received at her retirement party.

   _____

8. A <u>euphemism</u> is best used when you truly want to insult someone and be sure that person knows exactly how you feel.

   _____

*SHORT ANSWER:*   Write your answers on a separate sheet of paper.

1. Describe a situation in which you would want to <u>malign</u> someone.

2. If you had a secret <u>benefactor</u>, what would you like that person to do for you?

3. Describe the personality of a <u>benign</u> pet dog.

4. What might someone say during a <u>benediction</u>?

5. Describe your feelings if you are feeling <u>benevolent</u>.

6. What would you like someone to say about you in a <u>eulogy</u>?

7. What is the opposite of <u>malediction</u>?

8. What are <u>euphemisms</u> for the following words:

   dead _____

   stingy _____

   scrawny _____

   dumb _____

# Part B

 ***WORDS TO LEARN—SEE AND SAY***   Use the pronunciation guide on the first page of this book to help you SAY each word.

| 1. | loquacious | lō-kwā′shəs |
|---|---|---|
| 2. | retract | rĭ-trăkt′ |
| 3. | repercussion | rē′pər-kŭsh′ən |
| 4. | relinquish | rĭ-lĭng′kwĭsh |
| 5. | repudiate | rĭ-pyōō′dē-āt′ |
| 6. | revelation | rĕv′ə-lā′shən |
| 7. | dialogue | dī′ə-lôg′ |
| 8. | logophile | lŏgə-fīl′ |

 ***STRUCTURAL ELEMENTS***   Look at the structural elements of each word. Use these elements to unlock the word's meaning.

| re- | back, again |
|---|---|
| log, loq | words |

***CONTEXT CLUES***   Read the sentences. Use the words around the unfamiliar word to determine the word's meaning. Words in bold are the vocabulary words; words in italic are the context clues.

1. Although the twins looked very much alike, they were quite *different*. One was very **loquacious** while the other twin *barely would speak*.

2. After she found out who really said the maledictions about her, Sue had to **retract** the complaint she had filed with the Human Resources Department against her boss and *acknowledge she had blamed the wrong person.*

3. Bill will be dealing with **repercussions** for *many years following his arrest for underage drinking.*

4. Jayson's mother **relinquished**, *or gave up*, her responsibility for the family investments to her son. She could no longer handle the decisions due to her poor health.

5. The demand of the United States was for the United Nations to **repudiate** *and renounce* terrorism.

6. When the college president *announced* the plans to change the college's name, the **revelation** caught the faculty *by surprise*.

7. The children eavesdropped on their parents' **dialogue** in case they would *say* anything about their birthday presents.

8. You can tell I am a **logophile** because every spare corner of my *house is filled with books.*

 *DICTIONARY*    Read the following definitions.

1. **loquacious**   adjective

   **Etymology:** loq (words) ious (full of)

   Very talkative

   My third period class is very **loquacious** and I have a *hard time getting them to be quiet.*

   **Synonym:** verbose

   **Antonyms:** terse, quiet

2. **retract**   verb

   **Etymology:** re (back or again) tract (pull)

   To take something back

   I had to ask the newspaper to **retract** the *slanderous statement it printed about my character after it became clear that I was not the criminal.*

   **Synonym:** renege

   **Antonym:** protract

   **Vocabulary Tip:** Cats can retract their claws and some snakes can retract their fangs, but words spoken in anger can never be fully retracted, or taken back.

3. **repercussion**   noun

   **Etymology:** re (back, again) percuter (to strike)

   An often negative, indirect effect or consequence of an action; a rebound from an impact

   The **repercussion** of Anna's negative attitude *resulted in* her not getting the job she wanted.

   **Synonym:** reaction

   **Vocabulary Tip:** The word *repercussion* is commonly used in the plural. Repercussions can be thought of as a ripple effect occurring because of an incident or action. (www.vocabulary-vocabulary.com)

4. **relinquish**   verb

   **Etymology:** re (back, again) linquere (to leave)

   To cease holding physically; to let go; to surrender possession or right

   The attorney told his client that once the client **relinquishes** his rights to the property in dispute, he will *never be able to get it back.*

   **Synonyms:** abdicate, surrender

   **Antonym:** keep, retain

5. **repudiate**   verb

   **Etymology:** re (back, again) pudium (to cause shame)

   To cast away; to refuse to accept as true; to reject the validity or authority of

The mother of the convicted murderer **repudiated** the eyewitness account and *said it was inaccurate.*

**Synonym:** reject

**Antonym:** acknowledge

6. revelation   noun

**Etymology:** reveal (pull back the veil) tion (state, act or condition of)

A surprising piece of information that is displayed or made known

It was a complete **revelation** to Marcus when he *found out that* the sister he had grown up with was actually his niece.

**Synonyms:** insight, realization, disclosure, epiphany

**Antonyms:** secret, concealment

7. dialogue   noun

**Etymology:** dia (around) logue (words)

A conversation between two or more people

I recorded the **dialogue** *between a mother and her baby* for my child psychology class.

**Synonym:** conversation

8. logophile   noun

**Etymology:** logos (words) phile (one who loves)

One who loves words, books

My literature professor is a true **logophile**; she *treasures* each word in the *many books* that she reads.

**Synonym:** book lover

**Antonym:** bibliophobe

## *Practice Exercises*

### *MULTIPLE CHOICE*

1. When would it be appropriate to be <u>loquacious</u>?
   a. when watching a movie
   b. during a lecture class
   c. when you are meeting new people and trying to make them feel at ease
   d. when you are conducting a job interview and want to hear what the person being interviewed has to say

2. Which of the following is *not* a synonym for <u>retract</u>?
   a. withdraw
   b. back down
   c. take back
   d. brag

3. A possible <u>repercussion</u> for *not* balancing your checkbook is
   a. the inability to pay your monthly bills
   b. having extra money to go to a concert
   c. knowing exactly how much money you have
   d. the ability to help your friends who need money

4. Why would you <u>relinquish</u> your spot in a line to buy concert tickets?
    a. because you had enough hot chocolate and snacks to last all night
    b. because your best friend had a spot closer to the front
    c. because you enjoy talking to the other people in line
    d. because you sacrificed so much to be close to the front

5. How would a <u>repudiated</u> CEO be treated by the stockholders?
    a. asked to resign
    b. escorted out of jail
    c. given tickets to the annual ball
    d. receive a sincere apology from them

6. Which word fits best in this sentence: Joe's _____ that he had decided to change his major came as a complete surprise to his unsuspecting parents?
    a. message
    b. philosophy
    c. secret
    d. revelation

7. Which of the following do you need to have in order to have a <u>dialogue</u>?
    a. two or more people
    b. a topic of conversation
    c. the ability to somehow express your thoughts
    d. all of the above

8. What would you find in the home of someone who is a <u>logophile</u>?
    a. movies
    b. multiple televisions
    c. novels
    d. many board games

*FILL IN THE BLANK*   Select the BEST word for each sentence. Use each word only once.

| loquacious | retract | repercussions | relinquished |
| repudiated | dialogue | logophile | revelation |

1. When my car was hit from behind by a drunk driver, I tried to have a _____ with him about the accident, but he was not able to speak or think clearly.

2. Joe tried to _____ his proposal, but Sharon had already told all of her friends about the wedding.

3. The king _____ his throne after it was discovered that he had been stealing money from the treasury.

4. We want our daughter to grow up to be a _____, so we buy her new books for every holiday.

5. The _____ of not going to class were so severe that the student never missed a class.

6. The jury _____ the defendant's claim of innocence when they sentenced him to life in jail.

7. Ellie is so _____ that no one else can get a word in the conversation.

8. The _____ that Sue and Sam had eloped to Las Vegas was a shock to their parents.

*CORRECT OR INCORRECT?*   If the sentence is correct, write a "C" on the line provided. If not, write an "I" for incorrect, then REWRITE the sentence to make it correct. You can change any part of the sentence to make it correct.

1. I like peace and quiet, so the fact that my wife is <u>loquacious</u> suits me perfectly.

2. The <u>repercussion</u> of the accident was traced to bald tires that skidded on wet pavement.

   _____

3. When Dr. Jenkins noticed that his students had all fallen asleep, he <u>retracted</u> his offer of extra credit for watching the film.

   _____

4. The <u>repudiated</u> leader of the country was met with great respect when he addressed the other leaders of the government.

   _____

5. I was very happy when the purchase of my new home was completed and I <u>relinquished</u> ownership.

   _____

6. You can tell I am a <u>logophile</u> because on vacation all I want to do is watch movies.

   _____

7. It is important to have a <u>dialogue</u> with your son or daughter about the dangers of distracted driving when he or she is learning to drive.

   _____

8. The <u>revelation</u> that Jill was dating Jack was common knowledge.

   _____

*SHORT ANSWER*    Write your answers on a separate sheet of paper.

1. What are two positive and two negative aspects of having a friend who is <u>loquacious</u>?
2. What might you say if you insulted a friend and wanted to <u>retract</u> the statement?
3. Name two <u>repercussions</u> of missing too many classes.
4. Why might you <u>repudiate</u> the arguments of the president of the student organization?
5. What do you do if you <u>relinquish</u> control of your dog or cat to your sister?
6. What are three phrases that you could use to keep a <u>dialogue</u> going? One example could be "What happened next?"
7. Name two games that a <u>logophile</u> would like to play.
8. Think about your favorite movie or TV show. What <u>revelation</u> about one of the characters would surprise you? Not surprise you?

# Power Words

1. **eradicate**   ĭ-răd′ĭ-kāt′   verb

   To uproot; stamp out; destroy completely

   The destructive tornado **eradicated** everything in its path; *not one building was left standing.*

   **Synonyms:** destroy, obliterate, annihilate

   **Antonym:** grow

   **Memory Tip:** Note how *eradicate* sounds like "a rat in a crate." Now imagine you have a crate of belongings that has been infested with rats. You call an exterminator and say, "I will not be happy until every rat in the crate is eradicated. I don't want to see a single rat in the crate, so please do a good job and eradicate the rats." (www.vocabulary-vocabulary.com)

2. decimate   dĕs'ə-māt'   verb

   To destroy or kill a large part of a group; to inflict great destruction or damage

   The overabundance of deer **decimated** the farmer's freshly planted crops; *not one plant was left.*

   **Synonym:** destroy

   **Vocabulary Tip:** *Decimate* originally referred to the killing of every tenth person, a punishment used in the Roman army for mutinous legions. Today this meaning is commonly extended to include the killing of any large proportion of a group.

## Practice Exercises

1. Name two things you would like to <u>eradicate</u> (a) from your daily routine, (b) from the world, and (c) from your school.

2. What might have happened if a town were <u>decimated</u>?

# Chapter Review

## Extend Your Learning

Use one or more of the following exercises to practice the words in this chapter. Remember that it is important to use a variety of strategies in order to maximize your learning.

- Many of the words in this chapter have positive or negative meanings. Create a Venn diagram, and put the words that are positive on one side, the words that are negative on the other, and the words that have a neutral meaning in the overlapping portion.

- Form a group with other students and quiz each other on the words from this chapter. Make sure that everyone can pronounce the words correctly.

- Pick eight to ten words from this chapter. Use them in a short story or scenario about a crime and the legal proceedings that might follow. Stop short of the trial verdict. Share stories with others in your group and have them act as the jury and decide the verdict.

- Put the words from this chapter on index cards. Study the cards while exercising—either walking, on a stationary bike, or on a treadmill with a magazine rack.

## Expanded Word Forms

Select the appropriate word form for each of the sentences.

| | | |
|---|---|---|
| malign | maligned | maligning |
| benefactor | beneficiary | benevolent |

1. Scot is a kind and gentle person; his _____ personality has made him one of the most popular boys in his senior class. On the other hand, his sister has been accused of _____ Scot to just about everyone in the school.

2. Journalists have to be careful not to _____ someone in a newspaper or popular magazine. The person who was _____ has the right to sue for damages.

3. Mr. Jones was the _____ for many deprived young adults. He saw the need throughout the county and stepped in financially to help the young people become the _____ of his wealth.

*Puzzle Fun*

**Across**

2. Don't _____ your rights to the job until you find another one.
4. The young man presented a touching _____ at the funeral of his girlfriend.
6. It is very difficult to _____ some diseases but we must try.
7. Angie was very _____ so it was difficult to get an opportunity to express my ideas because she dominated the conversation.
10. Using offensive language and unkind comments is a form of _____
11. Bill Gates is a major _____ for many organizations that help young people.

**Down**

1. Andrew's _____ disposition made it very difficult for others to work with him.
2. The _____ from not doing homework or studying for exams was that Derrick failed the class.
3. The _____ offered by the senior class president at the awards dinner was heartfelt and genuine.
5. Jessica had to _____ everything that her boss said because he didn't have any basis for his remarks.
8. Jenna's _____ statement was taken in the wrong manner. She wanted to just express her feelings, but her coworkers took it to be the opposite.
9. After finding out that the grant was not awarded to her school, the public relations director had to _____ her statement that told the public that the school had been awarded the honor.

# CHAPTER ELEVEN

# Dedication to Learning
# New Vocabulary

*I know the price of success: dedication, hard work, and a
devotion to things you want to see happen.*

Frank Lloyd Wright, 1867–1959, architect

---

## CHAPTER OBJECTIVE

**Students will be able to identify and use words with the following common
structural elements:**

Roots: fac, fic
Prefixes: ambi-, ab-, ad-
Suffixes: -ist, -ian

---

## CHAPTER OUTLINE

💡 *Memory Tip*   Seeing the Big Picture—How Does Everything Fit Together?

🔍 *Learning Strategy*   Using the Internet as a Resource

**Part A**
*Words to Learn*

| | |
|---|---|
| facilitate | ambidextrous |
| fictitious | antagonist |
| ambiguous | lobbyist |
| ambivalent | theologian |

*Structural Elements*

| | |
|---|---|
| fac, fic | ambi- |
| -ist | -ian |

**Part B**
*Words to Learn*

| | |
|---|---|
| adversary | abscond |
| advent | aberrant |
| advocate | adjunct |
| absent | adjudicate |

*Structural Elements*

ab-, ad-

*Power Words*

| | |
|---|---|
| demeanor | causal |
| aesthetic | casual |

## Memory Tip    Seeing the Big Picture—How Does Everything Fit Together?

When learning information, your understanding and retention will be better if you can see the overall organization of the material. Once you understand the major structure, you can more easily learn the individual pieces and fit them in. In this textbook the words have been organized by common structural elements. It was easier to learn them because you learned the common elements and then expanded that to specific words.

You can apply this Memory Tip to your other courses. For example:

- When you are reading a textbook chapter, preview the chapter first to see the organization, and then start reading.

- When reviewing for an exam, look at all of your notes to identify the major topics to be covered on the exam, and then review all of the material under each topic.

- Preview each course syllabus at the beginning of the semester to see how the professor has organized the entire course. Once you understand the organization, you will have an easier time understanding each individual lecture.

## Learning Strategy    Using the Internet as a Resource

Educators have been trying to find the best way to help students gather information, analyze data, and evaluate findings. The Internet provides students the opportunity to analyze information effectively and efficiently. But it is important to be able to determine whether the information is valid/reliable and educationally sound.

The Internet offers students the ability to:

- Investigate real-world problems from any location in the world

- Find the most current information available

- Problem solve with others throughout the world

- Research endless problems or opportunities

Researchers have found that technology motivates students and encourages them to complete the task at hand. Students are more likely to create learning environments on a higher academic level, and they are more likely to go to greater depths in their research if using technology.

The question for students becomes, not whether the Internet should be used for information gathering, but rather how to evaluate particular websites for validity and reliability.

Students need to be concerned about the following criteria when using the Internet for investigation or research:

- *Purpose:* What is the purpose of the page? Is the page a commercial site, a government page, or strictly for entertainment?

- *Currency:* Is the page up-to-date? How can you determine the most current posting or update to the page?

- *Authority:* Who is the author? What are his or her credentials? Is there a reference list for this author?

- *Objectivity:* Does the content reflect a bias? If so, how does the bias impact the usefulness of the information?

- *Clarity:* Is the information clearly presented? Are the pages well-organized?

- *Appropriateness:* Is the content appropriate for the audience and the use? Is the content accurate and well-written?

# Part A

*WORDS TO LEARN—SEE AND SAY*    Use the pronunciation guide on the first page of this book to help you SAY each word.

1. facilitate          fə-sĭl′ĭ-tāt′

2. fictitious          fĭk-tĭsh′əs

3. ambiguous          ăm-bĭg′yo͞o-əs

4. ambivalent          ăm-bĭv′ə-lənt

5. ambidextrous        am-bi-′dek-strəs

6. antagonist          an-′ta-gə-nist

7. lobbyist            lŏb-ē-ist

8. theologian          thē′ə-lō-jən

 **STRUCTURAL ELEMENTS**    Look at the structural elements of each word. Use these elements to unlock the word's meaning.

fac             make or produce

fic             made up

ambi-           both

-ist            someone or something that

-ian            someone who

 **CONTEXT CLUES**    Read the sentences. Use the words around the unfamiliar word to determine the word's meaning. Words in bold are the vocabulary words; words in italic are the context clues.

1. There are many political arguments that have to be addressed in order to **facilitate**, *or help*, the withdrawal of troops in the Middle East.

2. Many musicians have **fictitious** names that are more appealing to their audience *than their given name.*

3. The **ambiguous** voice message that Mark left for Cindy was *confusing*; what was she to do—pick him up at the airport or at the bus station?

4. Stephanie felt **ambivalent** about going to the party; she really *didn't care whether she went or not.*

5. One of Joe's skills as a baseball player was that he was **ambidextrous**; he could bat *either right or left handed.*

6. The teacher knew that Billy was the **antagonist** and had *started the fight between the two boys.*

7. The **lobbyist** was *paid by the hotel to convince* the company executives to hold their yearly conference there.

8. Because I went to a college affiliated with my *church*, many of the professors in the Religious Studies Department were **theologians.**

 **DICTIONARY**    Read the following definitions.

1. **facilitate** verb

   **Etymology:** fac (make or produce) facili (easy) ate (to cause to be)

   To make easy or easier; to bring about

   Evan said he would **facilitate** the meeting between the two feuding parties, *keeping the conversation on target* and *not letting any arguments start.*

   **Synonyms:** help, assist, simplify

   **Antonym:** complicate

2. **fictitious** adjective

   **Etymology:** fic (made up) ious (full of or characteristic of)

   Of, relating to, or characterized by ficiton; imaginary; not genuinely believed or felt

The **fictitious** story that Mallory *made up* was easily detected by her teacher. Mrs. Smith clearly realized that Mallory didn't do her homework because she had been out late the prior evening.

**Synonyms:** made-up, fabricated

**Antonym:** truthful

3. ambiguous   adjective

**Etymology:** ambi (both, around) ious (full of or characteristic of)

Open to more than one interpretation

Mrs. Hill was *usually very clear* when giving directions, *although* she gave her students **ambiguous** instructions for the final project.

**Synonyms:** uncertain, obscure

**Antonyms:** certain, explicit, clear

4. ambivalent   adjective

**Etymology:** ambi (both, around) valentia (strength)

Feeling two different things about someone or something at the same time; uncertain or unable to decide what course to follow

I felt **ambivalent** about which job to take *because both offered unique opportunities.*

**Synonyms:** conflicting, contradictory

**Memory Tip:** Do not confuse the words *ambiguous* and *ambivalent*. The main difference is that *ambivalent* is used for people and their attitudes, whereas *ambiguous* refers to something said or written.

5. ambidextrous   adjective

**Etymology:** ambi (both) dexter (right hand—meaning right hand on both sides); -ous (full of or characteristic of)

Able to use both hands with equal facility; unusually skillful

It was very *unusual* to find an **ambidextrous** baseball player *because most of the time players favor one hand or the other* when batting and catching.

6. antagonist   noun

**Etymology:** ant (opposite or against) ist (someone who)

One who opposes or goes against another

The **antagonist** at my school is the one who constantly *goes against everything* the teacher and the other students want.

**Synonyms:** adversary, opponent

**Antonym:** protagonist, hero

7. lobbyist   noun

**Etymology:** lobby (lobby) -ist (person who)

A person acting for a special interest group to try to convince others

The **lobbyist** *for the athletic construction company* has been *trying to get the students to vote* for a new baseball field.

**Synonym:** representative

**Antonyms:** ally

8. theologian   noun

**Etymology:** theo (god or religion) ology (study or science of) ian (someone who)

Someone who studies gods or religions

*Father Mike* was a motivating **theologian** because he always made his remarks meaningful to the younger people in his *congregation*.

## *Practice Exercises*

### *MULTIPLE CHOICE*

1. Which of the following would <u>facilitate</u> buying a car?
   a. having to finance it yourself
   b. someone cosigning the loan with you
   c. an unpaid college loan
   d. not being able to decide which model you want

2. Why would you give a <u>fictitious</u> excuse about why you missed class?
   a. because you want to be truthful
   b. because you don't believe in lying
   c. because you want to keep the real reason a secret
   d. so that you do not get caught in a fib

3. What would you say if you were <u>ambivalent</u> about the new car your friend purchased?
   a. "It get greats gas milage."
   b. "I like the color and I like the style."
   c. "I wish it went better in the snow."
   d. "The seats are really comfortable but the gas milage is terrible."

4. Which of the following would the <u>antagonist</u> do in a play or movie?
   a. help people who were in trouble
   b. argue and work against the hero
   c. support the leading actress
   d. be the comic diversion

5. Which of the following might be the result of <u>ambiguous</u> information about a final exam?
   a. Students would not know what information would be covered.
   b. Students would know exactly what to study.
   c. Students would receive clear written instructions.
   d. Students would give the professor positive student evaluations.

6. Which of the following would be a unique skill characteristic of someone who is <u>ambidextrous</u>?
   a. be able to drive both a standard and an automatic transmission
   b. repeat back a long series of numbers he or she heard verbally
   c. write with both the right and left hands
   d. stand on one leg and touch one's nose with eyes closed

7. Which of the following is a statement that a <u>lobbyist</u> might say?
   a. "Do whatever you want."
   b. "Let's look at all sides of the issue."
   c. "I think the competitors have a good product that you should buy."
   d. "My company would like you to vote in our favor."

8. If you are a <u>theologian</u>, which course might you teach at the university?
   a. Plant and Animal Life of the Amazon
   b. Different Beliefs About God
   c. Baseball in America
   d. The Evolution of Las Vegas as a Center for Entertainment

*FILL IN THE BLANK*   Select the BEST word for each sentence. Use each word only once.

| facilitator | fictitious | ambiguous | ambivalent |
|---|---|---|---|
| antagonist | ambidextrous | lobbyist | theologian |

1. The part of the _____ in the senior class play was important because the character set up all of the discord and tension in the story line.

2. Joe was hired as a(n) _____ by the drug company. His job was to try to influence Congress to vote in favor of animal testing for new drugs.

3. Because Rob was interested in God and religion, he studied to become a(n) _____ in college.

4. The exam directions were so _____ that the students had no idea what the professor wanted.

5. The job of the group _____ was to keep the discussion on topic.

6. I had _____ feelings about the movie. There were some parts that I liked and other parts that I hated.

7. I don't know why I responded to the _____ email; I knew it wasn't real and was a scam.

8. One good thing about being _____ was that when I broke my right arm I was able to comb my hair with my left.

*CORRECT OR INCORRECT?*   If the sentence is correct, write a "C" on the line provided. If not, write an "I" for incorrect, then REWRITE the sentence to make it correct. You can change any part of the sentence to make it correct.

1. When my professor refused to tell me what was in the exam, he greatly <u>facilitated</u> my studying.

   _____

2. I registered for the credit card using a <u>fictitious</u> name and social security number because I only wanted the gift, not the credit card. Therefore, I was denied the card.

   _____

3. The professor's clearly well-planned and organized lectures made the students appreciate his <u>ambiguous</u> style.

   _____

4. The confident "A" student worked very hard; therefore, she was always <u>ambivalent</u> when it was time for grades to be posted.

   _____

5. I am <u>ambidextrous,</u> so when I broke my right arm I had to have help with writing essay exams.

   _____

6. Katie was the <u>antagonist</u> in the department and was the one who influenced everyone to get along with each other.

   _____

7. My sister is a <u>theologian</u> and is looking forward to studying the multiple species of fruit flies.

   _____

8. The <u>lobbyist</u>'s job was to help <u>facilitate</u> a balanced discussion to examine all possible sides of the issue.

   _____

*SHORT ANSWER*    Write your answers on a separate sheet of paper.

1. As a parent, how can you <u>facilitate</u> your child's transition from preschool to kindergarten

2. What is an example of a <u>fictitious</u> story? How can you tell whether a story is <u>fictitious</u> or not?

3. At your institution, what classes might be taught by a <u>theologian</u>?

4. What are some negatives and positives about having <u>lobbyists</u> work in Washington, DC?

5. Think of two of your favorite television shows. Identify the <u>antagonist</u> in each.

6. What kind of information are you getting if your professor gives you <u>ambiguous</u> feedback on your paper?

7. Name two things an <u>ambidextrous</u> person could do that a right- or left-handed person could not.

8. How do you feel if you are <u>ambivalent</u> about what restaurant to go to for dinner?

# Part B

 *WORDS TO LEARN—SEE AND SAY*    Use the pronunciation guide on the first page of this book to help you SAY each word.

1. adversary          ăd′vər-sĕr′ē

2. advent             ad′vĕnt′

3. advocate           ăd′və-kāt′

4. absent             ăb′sənt

5. abscond            ăb-skŏnd′

6. aberrant           ăb′ər-ənt

7. adjunct            ăj′ŭngkt′

8. adjudicate         ə-jōō′dĭ-kāt′

 *STRUCTURAL ELEMENTS*    Look at the structural elements of each word. Use these elements to unlock the word's meaning.

ab-              to be, away

ad-              toward, away

*CONTEXT CLUES*    Read the sentences. Use the words around the unfamiliar word to determine the word's meaning. Words in bold are the vocabulary words; words in italic are the context clues.

1. Dustin and Jerrod were in *competition for many years* as they were growing up. They remained **adversaries** even after high school and college.

2. On the college campus people hoped that the **advent** of the *new president would bring renewed* enthusiasm and excitement.

3. When the young boy entered school his **advocate** was *by his side to help smooth his way* through some rough spots.

4. Angela had been **absent** *from work for three days* without an excuse, so she will be given a written reprimand.

5. Bella decided to **abscond** *from the scene of the broken window* before her mother returned home from work and found her.

6. One **aberrant** gene has already been *linked to other social disorders*. Mallory's **aberrant**, *abnormal*, behavior caused her parents to suspect she was taking drugs.

7. As an **adjunct,** *or addition* to the assignment, the professor directed the students to analyze how they went about completing the assignment.

8. The college *judicial board* **adjudicated** nine cases during the semester *regarding cheating on exams.*

*DICTIONARY*    Read the following definitions.

1. adversary   noun

   **Etymology:** ad (away) ver (turn) -ary (something or someone)

   An enemy or opposition; an opponent

   At one time the two men were coworkers, even friends, *but after the heated argument* over a promotion they have become **adversaries**.

   **Synonyms:** opponent, antagonist

   **Antonyms:** proponent, supporter

2. advent   noun

   **Etymology:** ad (toward, away) vent (to come)

   The coming or arrival, especially of something extremely important

   The **advent** of *spring* meant the *flowers would soon be* in full bloom.

   **Synonym:** dawning

   **Antonym:** end

3. advocate   noun/verb

   **Etymology:** ad (toward) voc (voice, call) ate (state, act, or condition of)

   (noun) One that argues for a cause; a supporter or defender

   The court system uses several *professionals as children's* **advocates** for legal matters.

   (verb) To speak, plead, or argue in favor of

   Attorney Smith will **advocate** *for the disabled victim* pro bono, which means without charge.

   **Synonyms:** (noun) supporter; (verb) side with, back

4. absent   adjective/verb

   **Etymology:** ab (to be or away) sene (away)

   (adjective) Not present; missing; lost in thought; showing preoccupation

   To remember *those who were not with us*, we made a toast to our **absent** friends.

   (verb) To keep oneself away

   The judge had to **absent** himself from the case. He *could not preside* because the defendant was his brother.

   **Synonyms:** (adjective) away, missing; (verb) to distance

   **Antonyms:** (adjective) present; (verb) engaged

5. abscond   verb

   **Etymology:** ab (away or to be) condere (to put)

   To leave quickly and secretly and hide oneself, often to avoid arrest or prosecution

   *After he robbed the bank,* Jeffrey **absconded** *with the money* to avoid being caught.

   **Synonyms:** flee, escape

   **Antonyms:** return, stay

   **Vocabulary Tip:** *Abscond* is derived from the Latin *abscondere*, "to hide or put away." It usually carries a connotation of wrongdoing or secrecy.

6. aberrant    adjective

**Etymology:** ab (away or to be) errare (to wander)

Not normal or not what you would usually expect

The student's **aberrant** behavior was very *unusual and a surprise* to the teacher.

**Vocabulary Tip:** *Aberrant* and *abhorrent* are very different! *Aberrant* means "exceptionally or abnormally unusual" whereas *abhorrent* means "disgusting or detestable."

7. adjunct    adjective/noun

**Etymology:** ad (toward) junct (join)

(adjective) Attached or assigned as a temporary under another as in *adjunct faculty status*

The college has so many new freshman that it had to hire 30 **adjunct** faculty to fill the *teaching positions for the semester.*

(noun) Something added to something, therefore dependent upon

Matt's *short report* was **adjunct** *to the final term paper* that he would complete.

8. adjudicate    verb

**Etymology:** ad (toward) judi (judge) ate (to make or cause to be)

To listen and judge a case; to find a verdict

Three faculty members were selected to **adjudicate** *the case against* their colleague for plagiarism.

**Synonyms:** decide, determine

## *Practice Exercises*

### *MULTIPLE CHOICE*

1. What would you do with an <u>adversary</u>?
   a. work with him to solve a problem
   b. throw a surprise party for him
   c. compete against him in a sporting event
   d. nominate him for student government president

2. When would an <u>advent</u> happen?
   a. afterward as a period of reflection
   b. during an actual event
   c. leading up to or at the beginning
   d. whenever people wanted it to happen

3. Which of the following phrases might an <u>advocate</u> use?
   a. "This car has many new features that I think you will like."
   b. "Let me tell you about the needs in my hometown."
   c. "I will have a hamburger with tomato and lettuce."
   d. "Who do you think will win the baseball game tonight?"

4. If you <u>absent</u> yourself from a vote on new student policies you
   a. do not vote
   b. cast your vote and leave
   c. try to persuade others to vote the same way you plan to vote
   d. vote the same way as your best friend

5. If a bibliophile <u>absconded</u> with an autobiography, what probably happened?
   a. A book lover stole a book from the library.
   b. Books were donated to the library in memory of someone who died.
   c. A book lover started to work at the library but missed several days because of illness.
   d. Someone wrote the story of her life and hid it in the library.

6. Which of the following would be <u>aberrant</u> behavior for a one-year-old boy?
   a. crying when his mother leaves
   b. learning how to walk
   c. trying to feed himself with his fingers
   d. talking in complete sentences

7. Someone who is an <u>adjunct</u> in a position would
   a. be hired for a short period of time
   b. be next in line to be CEO
   c. be working on a volunteer basis and not get paid
   d. be entrenched in the inner workings of the company

8. In which of the following situations might a group of students <u>adjudicate</u> a concern?
   a. to decide the song of the week during freshman orientation
   b. voting for homecoming queen and king
   c. when voicing their concerns during a school board meeting
   d. in a mock trial during law school

*FILL IN THE BLANK*   Select the BEST word for each sentence. Use each word only once.

| adversary | advent | absent | advocate |
|---|---|---|---|
| abscond | aberrant | adjunct | adjudicate |

1. The _____ for the food bank went to the local government to ask for more financial support.

2. The young woman's _____ driving caught the notice of the police officer who then followed her to see whether there was a problem.

3. Joe was elected to the university judiciary council. The main duty of the council was to _____ cases of students having violated the code of conduct.

4. The _____ season right before the holidays was a time of preparation.

5. The _____ dog trainer was working at the kennel for one year to get experience while she went to school to become a veterinarian.

6. Joe was _____ so many times he failed the course.

7. If you _____ with a designer purse from the department store, you will be charged with shoplifting.

8. I tried very hard to beat my _____ on the tennis court.

*CORRECT OR INCORRECT?*   If the sentence is correct, write a "C" on the line provided. If not, write an "I" for incorrect, then REWRITE the sentence to make it correct. You can change any part of the sentence to make it correct.

1. The two <u>adversaries</u> were best friends and agreed on everything.

   _____

2. If you strongly believe in a cause, you might consider becoming an <u>advocate</u> and trying to convince government leaders to agree with your views.

   _____

3. The organizers met during the <u>advent</u> of the conference for a wrap-up session and debriefing.

_____

4. When I was on the student judiciary council, I had to <u>absent</u> myself from the hearing when my roommate was caught cheating.

_____

5. Because I did not want my elderly aunt to drive anymore, I <u>absconded</u> with her car keys.

_____

6. It is important for kindergarteners to learn how to get along in a group, so <u>aberrant</u> behavior is encouraged.

_____

7. The <u>adjunct</u> faculty member had a long-term contract and was named dean of the college.

_____

8. Bill received so many traffic citations that he had to appear before a judge to have his case <u>adjudicated</u>.

_____

*SHORT ANSWER*   Write your answers on a separate sheet of paper.

1. What is a current issue that you would consider being an <u>advocate</u> for? Why?
2. Describe an event or time in your life when you had an <u>adversary</u>; for example, during a tennis match.
3. What do you like best about the <u>advent</u> of fall? Of summer?
4. What are three common reasons students are <u>absent</u> from class?
5. When would it legal to <u>abscond</u> with something? Be creative!
6. What are three examples of normal behavior at a rock concert that might seem <u>aberrant</u> in the classroom?
7. What are the benefits of being hired in an <u>adjunct</u> position? Are there any negatives? If so, what?
8. If you were on the judiciary council at your institution, what types of cases would you <u>adjudicate</u>?

# Power Words

1. **demeanor**  dĭ-mē′nər  noun

   The way in which a person behaves; a person's outward behavior, manner, or appearance, especially as it reflects on mood or character

   Her **demeanor** was a dead giveaway that she was nervous. She kept *twisting in her seat and tapping her fingers on the table.*

   **Synonyms:** presence, attitude, conduct

2. **aesthetic**  ĕs-thĕt′ĭk  noun/adjective

   (noun) A guiding principle in matters of artistic beauty and taste; artistic sensibility

   Joel was proud of his **aesthetics**; he thought his *taste in art* was better than that of most people.

   (adjective) Of or concerning the appreciation of beauty or good taste

   The portrait had more than **aesthetic** beauty to Megan; it *also had sentimental value* because it was from the last picture taken of her great-grandfather.

   **Synonyms:** tasteful, artful

   **Antonym:** ugly

3. causal    kô′zəl    adjective

Indicative of or expressing a cause

A **causal** *relationship* exists *between* the *scarcity of a product and the demand,* thus the term "supply and demand."

4. casual    kăzh′ōō-əl    adjective

Informal, relaxed; happening by chance

The **casual** and *relaxed atmosphere* of the professor's home made the students feel comfortable when they met there.

**Synonym:** everyday

**Antonyms:** formal, stuffy

## *Practice Exercises*

1. What is the proper <u>demeanor</u> for a movie theater? For a football game? Why are they different?

2. Name something that you think has <u>aesthetic</u> value. Explain your answer.

3. What are the <u>causal</u> factors to your success in college?

4. Describe your favorite <u>casual</u> outfit. Why is it your favorite?

# Chapter Review

## *Extend Your Learning*

Use one or more of the following exercises to practice the words in this chapter. Remember that it is important to use a variety of strategies in order to maximize your learning.

• Construct concept maps to show how the words are related and also to display their different meanings.

• Study with one or more students from your class. Divide the words equally among the group and then verbally explain the meanings to each other. Be sure to use your own words and give an example of the meaning.

• The Memory Tip in this chapter was to see the big picture and understand how everything fits together. To do that with these words, construct one concept map and include all of the words from the chapter to see how they are related to each other. If there are any outliers (words that do not fit), make a note of them separately on the side of your paper.

• Read the words, definitions, and sample sentences into a voice recorder. Listen to the recording while you walk or do other physical activity.

## *Expanded Word Forms*

Select the appropriate word form for each of the sentences.

| facilitate | facilitating | facilitation | facilitator (use twice) | casual |
|---|---|---|---|---|
| casually | abscond | absconded | absconding | |

1. The _____ of the conference is an extremely important function. The _____ has the responsibility of making sure that the conference attendees and presenters have everything that they need.

2. _____ an icebreaker game at a party can be fun.

3. It is not easy to _____ a discussion involving a large group of people. The _____ must make sure that everyone has a chance to express his or her views.

4. Mike _____ with the exam answers when he saw them sticking out of the professor's briefcase. He knew it was wrong to _____ with the exam key. Because he was caught _____ with the answers, he was dismissed from the university.

5. Bill felt most comfortable when he was _____ dressed. He was very happy when his fiancé said he did not have to wear a tuxedo to the destination wedding in Mexico but could dress "beach _____."

*Puzzle Fun*

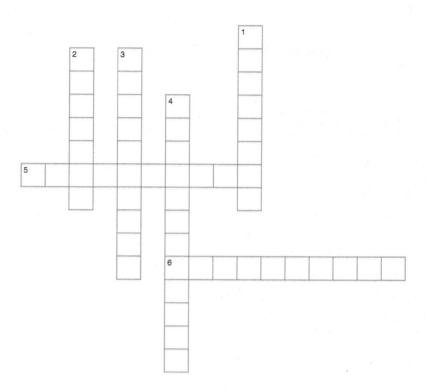

**Across**

5. The _____ story that Tyler told about the accident was very obvious to detect because he gave all the wrong information including the time and day of the incident.

6. When a _____ discusses religion and scriptures, it is assumed that he is very knowledgeable because he has had years of education.

**Down**

1. The _____ campaigned for three months to get the bill passed.

2. Mrs. Jones was just hired as a temporary or _____ teacher at my college.

3. Judge Judy does an excellent job when she has to _____ a case on TV. Not only is she fair but she is entertaining.

4. Ryan plays golf using his left hand but he writes with his right hand. That makes him truly _____.

# Appendix A

## ANSWERS TO MULTIPLE CHOICE QUESTIONS

### *Chapter Two*

**Part A:**  1. a   2. d   3. a   4. b   5. b   6. b   7. a
**Part B:**  1. c   2. a   3. a   4. c   5. c   6. a   7. b   8. c

### *Chapter Three*

**Part A:**  1. a   2. b   3. b   4. c   5. b   6. d   7. a   8. b   9. c
**Part B:**  1. a   2. b   3. c   4. d   5. a   6. c   7. b   8. a

### *Chapter Four*

**Part A:**  1. c   2. b   3. a   4. d   5. d   6. d   7. c
**Part B:**  1. b   2. a   3. c   4. d   5. a   6. b   7. d   8. d   9. d

### *Chapter Five*

**Part A:**  1. b   2. b   3. c   4. b   5. c   6. b   7. b
**Part B:**  1. b   2. b   3. d   4. c   5. a   6. d   7. a   8. a   9. b

### *Chapter Six*

**Part A:**  1. c   2. b   3. a   4. a   5. b   6. a   7. b
**Part B:**  1. c   2. d   3. a   4. b   5. a   6. d   7. d

### *Chapter Seven*

**Part A:**  1. a   2. c   3. b   4. b   5. c   6. b   7. c
**Part B:**  1. a   2. b   3. a   4. d   5. b   6. b   7. c

### *Chapter Eight*

**Part A:**  1. b   2. a   3. c   4. b   5. c   6. a   7. c   8. b
**Part B:**  1. b   2. c   3. c   4. a   5. d   6. b   7. c   8. d

### *Chapter Nine*

**Part A:**  1. c   2. b   3. d   4. a   5. d   6. a   7. a   8. d   9. c
**Part B:**  1. b   2. d   3. c   4. b   5. b   6. c   7. b   8. a

## *Chapter Ten*

**Part A:**   1. b    2. c    3. b    4. a    5. c    6. b    7. a    8. d    9. b
**Part B:**   1. c    2. d    3. a    4. b    5. a    6. d    7. d    8. c

## *Chapter Eleven*

**Part A:**   1. b    2. c    3. d    4. b    5. a    6. c    7. d    8. b
**Part B:**   1. c    2. c    3. b    4. a    5. a    6. d    7. a    8. a

# APPENDIX B

## WORD LIST WITH CHAPTER NUMBERS

| *Word* | *Chapter* | *Word* | *Chapter* |
|---|---|---|---|
| abbreviate | 5 | benevolent | 10 |
| aberrant | 11 | benign | 10 |
| abscond | 11 | bibliophile | 8 |
| absent | 11 | bilateral | 4 |
| adjudicate | 11 | casual | 11 |
| adjunct | 11 | catalyst | 4 |
| advent | 11 | catastrophe | 4 |
| adversary | 11 | causal | 11 |
| advocate | 11 | cohort | 2 |
| aesthetic | 11 | collaborate | 2 |
| agency | 9 | components | 2 |
| albatross | 6 | confer | 6 |
| ambidextrous | 11 | conformist | 2 |
| ambiguous | 11 | cognitive | 9 |
| ambivalent | 11 | congregate | 2 |
| ameliorate | 4 | connotative | 5 |
| analogy | 2 | consolidate | 2 |
| anarchy | 3 | contaminate | 2 |
| annotate | 8 | contend | 7 |
| anomalous | 3 | contraband | 9 |
| anomaly | 3 | controversy | 9 |
| anonymous | 6 | converge/convergence | 2 |
| antagonist | 11 | corroborate | 2 |
| antecedent | 7 | counterpart | 9 |
| anteroom | 7 | counterproductive | 9 |
| antiestablishment | 9 | deceptive | 5 |
| antisocial | 9 | decimate | 10 |
| antonym | 6 | decipher | 4 |
| apathy | 3 | deem | 7 |
| archetype | 3 | deference | 6 |
| aristocrat | 3 | demeanor | 11 |
| autobiography | 8 | democracy | 3 |
| autograph | 8 | demography | 8 |
| autonomy | 8 | demoralize | 4 |
| benediction | 10 | denotative | 5 |
| benefactor | 10 | detractor | 4 |

| Word | Chapter | Word | Chapter |
|------|---------|------|---------|
| dialogue | 10 | intrastate | 4 |
| eccentric | 5 | introvert | 8 |
| ecocide | 7 | lateral | 4 |
| egregious | 2 | lobbyist | 11 |
| embezzle | 5 | logophile | 10 |
| emigrate | 5 | loquacious | 10 |
| empathy | 5 | malediction | 10 |
| empirical | 6 | malefactor | 10 |
| emulate | 5 | malign | 10 |
| entrench | 5 | mandatory | 5 |
| eradicate | 10 | manipulate | 9 |
| eulogy | 10 | manual | 9 |
| euphemism | 10 | matricide | 7 |
| exhilarate | 5 | metacognition | 9 |
| exonerate | 5 | misogynist | 7 |
| extenuate | 5 | monarch | 3 |
| extrovert | 8 | morale | 2 |
| facilitate | 11 | narcissism | 6 |
| fervent | 4 | nominal | 6 |
| fictitious | 11 | nominate | 6 |
| fratricide | 7 | notorious | 2 |
| genesis | 7 | omnipotent | 3 |
| genetic | 7 | omnipresent | 3 |
| genocide | 7 | omniscient | 3 |
| graphology | 8 | omnivorous | 3 |
| gregarious | 2 | opulent | 4 |
| hierarchy | 3 | panacea | 3 |
| hyperbole | 3 | pandemonium | 3 |
| hyperthermia | 3 | panorama | 3 |
| hypothermia | 3 | paraphrase | 8 |
| hypothesis | 3 | pathology | 3 |
| immoral | 2 | patricide | 7 |
| impending | 5 | pedagogy | 8 |
| impetuous | 2 | pedestal | 8 |
| imply | 6 | pediatric | 8 |
| incognito | 9 | pedophile | 8 |
| induce | 7 | perspective | 5 |
| infer | 6 | pervasive | 5 |
| infiltrate | 5 | philosophy | 9 |
| insidious | 5 | physiological | 4 |
| integrate | 2 | podiatrist | 8 |
| interpersonal | 4 | podium | 8 |
| interval | 4 | postmortem | 7 |
| intramural | 4 | postpone | 7 |

| Word | Chapter | Word | Chapter |
|------|---------|------|---------|
| postscript | 6 | spectacle | 9 |
| predict | 7 | spectacular | 9 |
| prejudice | 7 | speculate | 9 |
| pseudonym | 6 | superfluous | 2 |
| pseudoscience | 6 | synonym | 6 |
| psychological | 4 | technophile | 8 |
| rationalize | 5 | terrarium | 4 |
| relinquish | 10 | theologian | 11 |
| repercussion | 10 | transcribe | 6 |
| repudiate | 10 | transfer | 6 |
| retract | 10 | transformation | 8 |
| revelation | 10 | transient | 8 |
| scribe | 6 | transmit | 8 |
| segregate | 2 | ubiquitous | 9 |
| solarium | 4 | unilateral | 4 |
| sophisticated | 9 | urgency | 9 |
| sophomore | 9 | vehement | 7 |